CAMBRIDGE SCHOOL

Shakespeare

King Lear

Edited by Elspeth Bain, Jonathan Morris and Rob Smith

Series Editor: Rex Gibson
Director, Shakespeare and Schools Project

CAMBRIDGE
UNIVERSITY PRESS

Published by the Press Syndicate of the University of Cambridge
The Pitt Building, Trumpington Street, Cambridge CB2 1RP
40 West 20th Street, New York, NY 10011–4211, USA
10 Stamford Road, Oakleigh, Melbourne 3166, Australia

First published 1996

Printed in Great Britain at the University Press, Cambridge

A catalogue record for this book is available from the British Library.

Library of Congress cataloguing in publication data applied for.

ISBN 0 521 46697 0

Designed by Richard Morris, Stonesfield Design
Picture research by Callie Kendall

Thanks are due to the following for permission to reproduce photographs:

Jacket: by courtesy of the board of trustees of the National Museums & Galleries on Merseyside
(Walker Art Gallery); 4, 55, 72, 120, 221, 229, 230*t*, Shakespeare Centre Library, Stratford-upon-
Avon; 14, 44, 144, 188, Angus McBean/print by Shakespeare Centre Library, Stratford-upon-
Avon; 94, 97, 133, 154, 170, 173, 196, 215, 217, 219, 222, © Donald Cooper/Photostage; 130, 194,
Joe Cocks Studio Collection/Shakespeare Centre Library, Stratford-upon-Avon; 180, courtesy of
BFI/Corinth Films; 230*b*, The Hungarian Theatre Centre, Budapest; 231*t*, courtesy of Columbia
Pictures/Tristar Pictures/Columbia Tristar Int 1 Television; Copyright 1996 Columbia Pictures
Industries Inc./print courtesy of BFI; 231*b*, Herald Ace-Nippon-Herald-Greenwich/Orion 1985,
courtesy of Kobal Collection

Contents

Cambridge School Shakespeare

This edition of *King Lear* is part of the *Cambridge School Shakespeare* series. Like every other play in the series, it has been specially prepared to help all students in schools and colleges.

This *King Lear* aims to be different from other editions of the play. It invites you to bring the play to life in your classroom, hall or drama studio through enjoyable activities that will increase your understanding. Actors have created their different interpretations of the play over the centuries. Similarly, you are encouraged to make up your own mind about *King Lear*, rather than having someone else's interpretation handed down to you.

Cambridge School Shakespeare does not offer you a cut-down or simplified version of the play. This is Shakespeare's language, filled with imaginative possibilities. You will find on every left-hand page: a summary of the action, an explanation of unfamiliar words, a choice of activities on Shakespeare's language, characters and stories.

Between each act and in the pages at the end of the play, you will find notes, illustrations and activities. This will help to increase your understanding of the whole play.

There are a large number of activities to give you the widest choice to suit your own particular needs. Please don't think you have to do every one. Choose the activities that will help you most.

This edition will be of value to you whether you are studying for an examination, reading for pleasure, or thinking of putting on the play to entertain others. You can work on the activities on your own or in groups. Many of the activities suggest a particular group size, but don't be afraid to make up larger or smaller groups to suit your own purposes.

Although you are invited to treat *King Lear* as a play, you don't need special dramatic or theatrical skills to do the activities. By choosing your activities, and by exploring and experimenting, you can make your own interpretations of Shakespeare's language, characters and stories. Whatever you do, remember that Shakespeare wrote his plays to be acted, watched and enjoyed.

Rex Gibson

This edition of *King Lear* uses the text of the play established by Jay L. Halio in *The New Cambridge Shakespeare*.

List of characters

The Royal House of Britain

LEAR king of Britain
GONERILL his eldest daughter
REGAN his second daughter
CORDELIA his youngest daughter
THE DUKE OF ALBANY married to Gonerill
THE DUKE OF CORNWALL married to Regan

The Gloucester family

THE EARL OF GLOUCESTER
EDGAR his elder son and heir
EDMOND his illegitimate son

Other characters in the play

FOOL
THE EARL OF KENT (later disguised as CAIUS) } in the king's service

THE KING OF FRANCE
THE DUKE OF BURGUNDY } suitors to Cordelia

OSWALD Gonerill's steward
CURAN a courtier
A GENTLEMAN
AN OLD MAN Gloucester's tenant
A CAPTAIN
A HERALD
A SERVANT in Cornwall's household

Knights, gentlemen, soldiers, attendants, messengers, servants

The action of the play takes place in various parts of the kingdom of Britain.

Discussing King Lear's plan to abdicate and share out his kingdom, Kent and Gloucester are unsure about which of his two sons-in-law Lear prefers. Gloucester introduces Edmond, his illegitimate son.

1 Prediction

Sometimes a playwright suggests the themes of a play right at the start. Identify the main topics of conversation in the script opposite, and use them to make some predictions about how you think the play will develop. Write three sentences summarising your predicted story.

2 'Do you smell a fault?' (in pairs)

Gloucester's frank account of Edmond's conception and birth (lines 11–13) seems to provoke a non-verbal reaction from Kent at line 13. Kent may be shocked by Gloucester's story of his sexual conquest, or he may feel embarrassed for Edmond. As Gloucester and Kent, decide how you would speak and react to Gloucester's 'Do you smell a fault?'.

3 Gloucester gossips … Edmond listens (in groups of three)

Edmond hears himself described as the result of one of his father's sexual adventures, as a 'knave' and a 'whoreson'. He learns that he will soon be sent away again. But do you think Gloucester is speaking inconsiderately, or with humour and affection?

Take parts and speak lines 7–28. Swap roles and read the lines again, so that each person can try a different way of speaking Gloucester's words: discreetly, furtively, jokingly, boastfully, or in some other way. Afterwards, talk together about your impressions of Gloucester, and about what Edmond may be thinking in response to his father's conversation with Kent.

---

affected favoured
**for qualities are so … either's
  moiety** their merits are so evenly
  balanced, no one can predict what
  share of the kingdom they will
  receive
brazed to't hardened to it

issue result
by order of law born within
  marriage
whoreson bastard, son of a
  prostitute
out nine years away for nine years

The tragedy of King Lear

ACT I SCENE I
King Lear's palace

Enter KENT, GLOUCESTER, *and* EDMOND

KENT I thought the king had more affected the Duke of Albany than Cornwall.

GLOUCESTER It did always seem so to us: but now in the division of the kingdom, it appears not which of the dukes he values most, for qualities are so weighed that curiosity in neither can make choice of either's moiety. 5

KENT Is not this your son, my lord?

GLOUCESTER His breeding, sir, hath been at my charge. I have so often blushed to acknowledge him, that now I am brazed to't.

KENT I cannot conceive you. 10

GLOUCESTER Sir, this young fellow's mother could; whereupon she grew round wombed, and had indeed, sir, a son for her cradle ere she had a husband for her bed. Do you smell a fault?

KENT I cannot wish the fault undone, the issue of it being so proper.

GLOUCESTER But I have a son, sir, by order of law, some year elder 15 than this, who yet is no dearer in my account; though this knave came something saucily to the world before he was sent for, yet was his mother fair, there was good sport at his making, and the whoreson must be acknowledged. Do you know this noble gentleman, Edmond? 20

EDMOND No, my lord.

GLOUCESTER My lord of Kent; remember him hereafter as my honourable friend.

EDMOND My services to your lordship.

KENT I must love you and sue to know you better. 25

EDMOND Sir, I shall study deserving.

GLOUCESTER He hath been out nine years, and away he shall again. The king is coming.

Lear intends to divide Britain between his daughters. He sets them a test: whoever expresses the greatest love will be given the largest portion. Gonerill voices limitless love for him and wins a share.

From left to right: Cornwall, Regan, Gonerill, Lear, Cordelia and Albany. What do you think is the significance of the sword?

1 The royal 'we'

Monarchs often use the plural 'we' and 'our' instead of 'I' and 'my'. Speak lines 31–49, pointing at yourself each time Lear refers to himself.

Sennet trumpet fanfare
son son-in-law
constant will firm intention
several dowers separate marriage gifts
amorous sojourn visit as suitors
divest us both of part with

bounty generosity
nature ... challenge natural affection and good qualities are well matched
bounds limits, boundaries
champains plains
meads meadows

Sennet. Enter KING LEAR, CORNWALL, ALBANY, GONERILL,
     REGAN, CORDELIA, *and Attendants*

LEAR Attend the lords of France and Burgundy, Gloucester.
GLOUCESTER I shall, my lord.   *Exit*   30
LEAR Meantime we shall express our darker purpose.
          Give me the map there. Know, that we have divided
          In three our kingdom, and 'tis our fast intent
          To shake all cares and business from our age,
          Conferring them on younger strengths while we   35
          Unburdened crawl toward death. Our son of Cornwall,
          And you, our no less loving son of Albany,
          We have this hour a constant will to publish
          Our daughters' several dowers, that future strife
          May be prevented now. The princes, France and
              Burgundy,   40
          Great rivals in our youngest daughter's love,
          Long in our court have made their amorous sojourn,
          And here are to be answered. Tell me, my daughters
          (Since now we will divest us both of rule,
          Interest of territory, cares of state),   45
          Which of you shall we say doth love us most,
          That we our largest bounty may extend
          Where nature doth with merit challenge? Gonerill,
          Our eldest born, speak first.
GONERILL Sir, I love you more than word can wield the matter,   50
          Dearer than eyesight, space, and liberty;
          Beyond what can be valued, rich or rare,
          No less than life, with grace, health, beauty, honour;
          As much as child e'er loved, or father found;
          A love that makes breath poor, and speech unable;   55
          Beyond all manner of so much I love you.
CORDELIA [*Aside*] What shall Cordelia speak? Love, and be silent.
LEAR Of all these bounds even from this line, to this,
          With shadowy forests and with champains riched
          With plenteous rivers and wide-skirted meads,   60
          We make thee lady. To thine and Albany's issues
          Be this perpetual. What says our second daughter,
          Our dearest Regan, wife of Cornwall?

5

Regan claims that her greatest joy is her father's love. Lear gives her land equal to Gonerill's share. Cordelia refuses to join in the love test, saying that she simply loves her father as a daughter should.

1 'Nothing' (in pairs)

If she speaks pleasingly, as her father wishes, Cordelia, Lear's 'joy', will win the richest third of the kingdom (lines 80–1). But she refuses to compete with her sisters' flattery. While they offer exaggerated praise, she answers Lear's request for a declaration of love with 'nothing', a word which will be used repeatedly throughout the play. Should Cordelia speak quietly and politely, or loudly and emphatically for all to hear? Does Lear respond with instant rage or with embarrassed patience? In one production, Lear and his courtiers thought Cordelia was joking and laughed indulgently at her words.

Take parts and speak lines 80–102 in various ways to discover which interpretation you prefer.

2 Cordelia's explanation (in pairs)

In lines 90–8, Cordelia explains that she loves Lear according to her duties as a daughter. She also casts doubt on the sincerity of her sisters' extravagant praise. If they love Lear totally, why do they have husbands? Cordelia says that when she marries, her love will be divided between her husband and her father.

a One person speaks Cordelia's lines 90–8. At each mark of punctuation, the partner interrupts with one of Lear's lines at 85, 89–90 or 99. Cordelia tries to make her message clear and persuasive, despite the frequent interruptions. Lear tries to show the different emotions he feels.

b Contrast Cordelia's lines 90–8 with Gonerill's and Regan's declaration of love for Lear. Talk together about what the contrast suggests about the differing personalities of the sisters and about their attitudes to their father.

---

self-mettle same spirit
square of sense human body, perfect feeling
felicitate happy
ponderous heavy, valuable
validity value
interested admitted, married

opulent rich
bond duty as a daughter
mar damage
begot fathered
take my plight accept my wedding vow

REGAN I am made of that self-mettle as my sister
    And prize me at her worth. In my true heart   65
    I find she names my very deed of love.
    Only she comes too short, that I profess
    Myself an enemy to all other joys
    Which the most precious square of sense possesses,
    And find I am alone felicitate   70
    In your dear highness' love.
CORDELIA [*Aside*]   Then poor Cordelia,
    And yet not so, since I am sure my love's
    More ponderous than my tongue.
LEAR To thee and thine hereditary ever
    Remain this ample third of our fair kingdom,   75
    No less in space, validity, and pleasure
    Than that conferred on Gonerill. Now our joy,
    Although our last and least, to whose young love
    The vines of France and milk of Burgundy
    Strive to be interessed. What can you say to draw   80
    A third more opulent than your sisters? Speak.
CORDELIA Nothing, my lord.
LEAR Nothing?
CORDELIA Nothing.
LEAR Nothing will come of nothing, speak again.   85
CORDELIA Unhappy that I am, I cannot heave
    My heart into my mouth: I love your majesty
    According to my bond, no more nor less.
LEAR How, how, Cordelia? Mend your speech a little,
    Lest you may mar your fortunes.
CORDELIA   Good my lord,   90
    You have begot me, bred me, loved me. I
    Return those duties back as are right fit,
    Obey you, love you, and most honour you.
    Why have my sisters husbands, if they say
    They love you all? Happily, when I shall wed,   95
    That lord whose hand must take my plight shall carry
    Half my love with him, half my care and duty.
    Sure, I shall never marry like my sisters.
LEAR But goes thy heart with this?
CORDELIA   Ay, my good lord.

Enraged, Lear disowns Cordelia and divides her inheritance between Gonerill and Regan. He proposes that he and his one hundred knights live with Gonerill and Regan in turn. Kent protests.

1 Cursing Cordelia (in large groups)

In lines 102–14, Lear invokes ancient beliefs to curse and reject Cordelia. He is bitterly angry at her unwillingness to declare unqualified love for him. Here's one way to help you explore the force of Lear's rage and its effect on Cordelia. One person (volunteer only!) plays Cordelia. The others stand in a circle around her. Each one chooses a short section of Lear's words which they feel conveys his rejection of Cordelia. This extract can be five or six words, or as much as three lines. In turn, speak the words you have chosen. When you have spoken your words, turn your back on Cordelia. Repeat the activity, adding suitable gestures to illustrate your words. Cordelia can try ways of gesturing and speaking lines from earlier in the script to respond to these attacks, but may not leave the circle.

After you have tried several versions of the activity, talk together about the way in which the language expresses Lear's feelings and the effect it has on Cordelia.

2 The king's commands

Lear asserts his authority in lines 115–33. He issues orders and proclaims his intentions. But to whom? Work through the lines, a sentence or small section at a time, identifying the person being addressed.

3 What's your choice?

Line 137 may mean 'stop blathering and get to the point' or 'I've made up my mind. Shut up or I'll make you suffer'. Which do you prefer and why?

Hecate goddess of witchcraft
operation of the orbs astrological influence of the stars
Propinquity and property closeness and relationship
Scythian cruel savage

makes his generation messes eats his children (messes = meals)
Pre-eminence high status
th'addition titles, honours
sway control
coronet crown (see cover picture)

LEAR So young, and so untender?   100
CORDELIA So young, my lord, and true.
LEAR Let it be so, thy truth then be thy dower.
       For by the sacred radiance of the sun,
       The mysteries of Hecate and the night,
       By all the operation of the orbs   105
       From whom we do exist and cease to be,
       Here I disclaim all my paternal care,
       Propinquity and property of blood,
       And as a stranger to my heart and me
       Hold thee from this forever. The barbarous Scythian,   110
       Or he that makes his generation messes
       To gorge his appetite, shall to my bosom
       Be as well neighboured, pitied, and relieved,
       As thou my sometime daughter.
KENT   Good my liege –
LEAR Peace, Kent,   115
       Come not between the dragon and his wrath.
       I loved her most, and thought to set my rest
       On her kind nursery. Hence and avoid my sight!
       So be my grave my peace, as here I give
       Her father's heart from her. Call France. Who stirs?   120
       Call Burgundy. – Cornwall and Albany,
       With my two daughters' dowers digest the third.
       Let pride, which she calls plainness, marry her.
       I do invest you jointly with my power,
       Pre-eminence, and all the large effects   125
       That troop with majesty. Ourself by monthly course,
       With reservation of an hundred knights
       By you to be sustained, shall our abode
       Make with you by due turn; only we shall retain
       The name and all th'addition to a king: the sway,   130
       Revenue, execution of the rest,
       Beloved sons, be yours; which to confirm,
       This coronet part between you.
KENT   Royal Lear,
       Whom I have ever honoured as my king,
       Loved as my father, as my master followed,   135
       As my great patron thought on in my prayers –
LEAR The bow is bent and drawn, make from the shaft.

Kent challenges Lear's decisions. Kent swears loyalty, but continues to criticise the king's actions. Lear warns Kent to stop his protest on pain of death. Lear is furious, and begins to declare Kent's punishment.

1 Kent's plain speaking (in pairs)

In lines 138–48, Kent accuses Lear of madness, criticises the older daughters' empty flattery, urges Lear to hold on to power and defends Cordelia's sincerity. He addresses Lear as 'thou', an inappropriately intimate term for a subject to use to his monarch (who would expect the courtesy of the plural 'you').

One student speaks Kent's lines while the other, as Lear, moves around the room, changing direction as often as he wants. Kent must keep reading aloud, following Lear as closely as possible to make him listen. Lear must stop and turn round when Kent says something which bites deep into his feelings as a king and father. Afterwards, talk together about which of Kent's remarks you think Lear would find the most hurtful.

2 Lear versus Kent (in pairs)

Work out ways of bringing out the tension and conflict between Lear and Kent in lines 149–61. For example, you could use pauses or speak very quickly without pausing. (It is a theatrical convention that when a line is shared, there is no pause between speakers.)

3 Loyal Kent ... the 'true blank'

Sight and blindness will become key themes in the play. In lines 152–3, Kent implores Lear to 'See better', and offers to act as 'The true blank of thine eye'. The 'blank' could be the centre of a target or the line of sight. Imagine that the actor playing Kent asks you, 'Does it mean here that Lear should always keep Kent in view, or does it mean that Kent is the model of an honest truth-teller, or what ...?' Make your reply.

---

fork arrow-head
Reserve thy state keep your powers
Reverb no hollowness do not echo like an empty vessel
wage stake, make war
Apollo god of the sun

vassal wretched slave
Miscreant unbeliever, scoundrel
forbear stop
Revoke cancel, alter
vent clamour make noise
recreant traitor

KENT Let it fall rather, though the fork invade
　　　　The region of my heart. Be Kent unmannerly
　　　　When Lear is mad. What wouldst thou do, old man?　　140
　　　　Think'st thou that duty shall have dread to speak
　　　　When power to flattery bows? To plainness honour's
　　　　　　bound,
　　　　When majesty falls to folly. Reserve thy state,
　　　　And in thy best consideration check
　　　　This hideous rashness. Answer my life, my judgement:　　145
　　　　Thy youngest daughter does not love thee least,
　　　　Nor are those empty-hearted whose low sounds
　　　　Reverb no hollowness.
LEAR　　　　　　　　　　　　Kent, on thy life no more.
KENT My life I never held but as a pawn
　　　　To wage against thine enemies, ne'er feared to lose it,　　150
　　　　Thy safety being motive.
LEAR　　　　　　　　　　　　Out of my sight!
KENT See better, Lear, and let me still remain
　　　　The true blank of thine eye.
LEAR Now by Apollo –
KENT　　　　　　　　Now by Apollo, king,
　　　　Thou swear'st thy gods in vain.
LEAR　　　　　　　　　　　　O vassal! Miscreant!　　155
ALBANY, CORNWALL Dear sir, forbear.
KENT Kill thy physician, and thy fee bestow
　　　　Upon the foul disease. Revoke thy gift,
　　　　Or whilst I can vent clamour from my throat,
　　　　I'll tell thee thou dost evil.
LEAR　　　　　　　　　　　Hear me, recreant,　　160
　　　　On thine allegiance hear me.
　　　　That thou hast sought to make us break our vows,
　　　　Which we durst never yet; and with strained pride,
　　　　To come betwixt our sentence and our power,
　　　　Which nor our nature nor our place can bear,　　165
　　　　Our potency made good, take thy reward.
　　　　Five days we do allot thee for provision
　　　　To shield thee from disasters of the world,

Lear banishes Kent from Britain, threatening execution if he remains. Kent praises Cordelia's honesty, and urges Gonerill and Regan to fulfil their words of love. Lear offers Cordelia in marriage to Burgundy, without a dowry.

1 Kent's parting words

Enraged by Kent's plain speaking, Lear banishes him. Kent must leave Britain in six days. If he is still in the kingdom after ten days, he will be executed. In lines 174–81, Kent welcomes banishment if Lear is to act so tyrannically. Before he leaves, he addresses Lear, Cordelia and her sisters in turn, speaking in rhyming couplets. Write responses in the same style for Lear, Cordelia, Gonerill and Regan.

2 Choose the speaker

No one is really sure whether Shakespeare intended line 182 to be spoken by Cordelia, Gloucester or Cornwall. Which speaker would you choose to deliver the line? Give reasons for your choice.

3 Cordelia's price (in pairs)

a Lear speaks about Cordelia as though she were a thing of little saleable value. Take turns to speak lines 190–5, emphasising Cordelia's lack of worth, treating your partner as Cordelia, the object of your scorn.

b 'Take her or leave her?' In lines 196–8, Lear states the five conditions on which he will give Cordelia to Burgundy. How do you think she feels about being discussed by Lear and Burgundy as if she were a commodity? Imagine that, at the end of each condition (after each of the first five commas), Cordelia speaks an aside. What might she say?

---

trunk body
Jupiter ruler of the gods
large speeches grand words
Flourish trumpet fanfare
rivalled competed
present dower marriage gift
tender offer, give

aught anything
little seeming substance small
  deceptive thing
pieced added
fitly like suitably please
owes possesses

And on the sixth to turn thy hated back
Upon our kingdom; if on the tenth day following   170
Thy banished trunk be found in our dominions,
The moment is thy death. Away! By Jupiter,
This shall not be revoked.
KENT Fare thee well, king, since thus thou wilt appear,
    Freedom lives hence, and banishment is here.   175
    [*To Cordelia*] The gods to their dear shelter take thee,
      maid,
    That justly think'st and hast most rightly said.
    [*To Gonerill and Regan*] And your large speeches may your
      deeds approve,
    That good effects may spring from words of love.
    Thus Kent, O princes, bids you all adieu,   180
    He'll shape his old course in a country new.   *Exit*

Flourish. Enter GLOUCESTER *with* FRANCE *and* BURGUNDY [*and*]
Attendants

CORDELIA Here's France and Burgundy, my noble lord.
LEAR My lord of Burgundy,
    We first address toward you, who with this king
    Hath rivalled for our daughter. What in the least   185
    Will you require in present dower with her,
    Or cease your quest of love?
BURGUNDY   Most royal majesty,
    I crave no more than hath your highness offered,
    Nor will you tender less?
LEAR   Right noble Burgundy,
    When she was dear to us, we did hold her so,   190
    But now her price is fallen. Sir, there she stands.
    If aught within that little seeming substance,
    Or all of it, with our displeasure pieced
    And nothing more, may fitly like your grace,
    She's there, and she is yours.
BURGUNDY   I know no answer.   195
LEAR Will you with those infirmities she owes,
    Unfriended, new adopted to our hate,
    Dowered with our curse, and strangered with our oath,
    Take her, or leave her?

Burgundy declines Lear's conditions. Lear advises France to reject Cordelia.
France expresses amazement at Lear's sudden rejection of Cordelia. She asks
Lear to reveal that she has been condemned only for speaking honestly.

1 Making eye contact (in groups of three)

Take parts as France, Cordelia and Lear. France speaks lines 207–17
twice, first looking at Lear the whole time, and then gazing at Cordelia,
ignoring the king. How might France's different attempts at eye contact
alter the way Lear and Cordelia react to his words?

Work through Cordelia's lines 218–28, suggesting who she looks at as
she speaks each line.

The Duke of Burgundy rejects Cordelia.

Election choice
stray departure
T'avert to redirect
argument subject, theme
balm comfort

dismantle strip away
fore-vouched previously promised
reason without ... in me only a
  miracle could make me believe
still-soliciting eye always begging

BURGUNDY   Pardon me, royal sir,
　　　　Election makes not up in such conditions.   200
LEAR Then leave her, sir, for by the power that made me,
　　　　I tell you all her wealth. [*To France*] For you, great king,
　　　　I would not from your love make such a stray
　　　　To match you where I hate; therefore beseech you
　　　　T'avert your liking a more worthier way   205
　　　　Than on a wretch whom nature is ashamed
　　　　Almost t'acknowledge hers.
FRANCE   This is most strange,
　　　　That she whom even but now was your best object,
　　　　The argument of your praise, balm of your age,
　　　　The best, the dearest, should in this trice of time   210
　　　　Commit a thing so monstrous to dismantle
　　　　So many folds of favour. Sure, her offence
　　　　Must be of such unnatural degree
　　　　That monsters it, or your fore-vouched affection
　　　　Fall into taint; which to believe of her   215
　　　　Must be a faith that reason without miracle
　　　　Should never plant in me.
CORDELIA I yet beseech your majesty –
　　　　If for I want that glib and oily art,
　　　　To speak and purpose not, since what I well intend,   220
　　　　I'll do't before I speak – that you make known
　　　　It is no vicious blot, murder, or foulness,
　　　　No unchaste action or dishonoured step
　　　　That hath deprived me of your grace and favour,
　　　　But even for want of that for which I am richer –   225
　　　　A still-soliciting eye, and such a tongue
　　　　That I am glad I have not, though not to have it,
　　　　Hath lost me in your liking.
LEAR   Better thou
　　　　Hadst not been born than not t'have pleased me better.

Burgundy offers to marry Cordelia if Lear will guarantee the previously promised dowry. Lear refuses, and Burgundy rejects Cordelia. France takes her as his wife. Lear disowns Cordelia, and vows never to see her again.

1 'Nothing'

Lear's 'nothing' in line 240 echoes Cordelia's response to the love test. Suggest different ways in which Lear could speak 'nothing' here.

2 Cordelia interrupts

Realising that he is not going to gain a rich dowry, Burgundy rejects Cordelia. Cordelia interrupts the all-male discussion of her future to voice her own feelings about Burgundy: if you love status and wealth so much, I am not the right wife for you. Try speaking lines 242–4 angrily, forgivingly, dismissively or in other ways.

3 Paradoxical truths (in groups of five to seven)

France describes the strange way Cordelia's fortunes are working out. Lines 245–56 contain seven or eight antitheses (oppositions or paradoxes, for example 'rich'/'poor', 'losest'/'find'). Identify the antitheses and prepare a presentation of the lines with one person reading and the others miming. The first mime represents 'rich' changing into 'poor', and so on.

4 Who's who?

The painting by Ford Madox Brown (1821–93) on the cover of this edition illustrates lines 257–60. Identify who's who (France is not shown).

---

tardiness in nature natural reticence
history inner thoughts, story
regards other considerations
th'entire point the essential issue
respect and fortunes status and wealth
kindle warm, ignite

inflamed respect passionate admiration
waterish weak
unprized unvalued
though unkind even though they've been cruel and unsisterly
benison blessing

FRANCE Is it but this? A tardiness in nature,   230
        Which often leaves the history unspoke
        That it intends to do? My lord of Burgundy,
        What say you to the lady? Love's not love
        When it is mingled with regards that stands
        Aloof from th'entire point. Will you have her?   235
        She is herself a dowry.
BURGUNDY   Royal king,
        Give but that portion which yourself proposed,
        And here I take Cordelia by the hand,
        Duchess of Burgundy.
LEAR Nothing, I have sworn; I am firm.   240
BURGUNDY I am sorry then, you have so lost a father
        That you must lose a husband.
CORDELIA   Peace be with Burgundy;
        Since that respect and fortunes are his love,
        I shall not be his wife.
FRANCE Fairest Cordelia, that art most rich being poor,   245
        Most choice forsaken, and most loved despised,
        Thee and thy virtues here I seize upon.
        Be it lawful I take up what's cast away.   .
        Gods, gods! 'Tis strange, that from their cold'st neglect
        My love should kindle to inflamed respect.   250
        Thy dowerless daughter, king, thrown to my chance,
        Is queen of us, of ours, and our fair France.
        Not all the dukes of waterish Burgundy
        Can buy this unprized precious maid of me.
        Bid them farewell, Cordelia, though unkind;   255
        Thou losest here a better where to find.
LEAR Thou hast her, France, let her be thine; for we
        Have no such daughter, nor shall ever see
        That face of hers again. Therefore be gone,
        Without our grace, our love, our benison.   260
        Come, noble Burgundy.

        Flourish. Exeunt [Lear, Burgundy, Cornwall, Albany, Gloucester,
                    Edmond, and Attendants]

FRANCE   Bid farewell to your sisters.

Cordelia, doubting her sisters' sincerity, asks them to care for Lear. They scorn her words and prospects. Left together, Gonerill and Regan fear Lear's rash judgement, and resolve to work together to control him.

1 Three sisters (in groups of three)

How do the sisters speak their farewell conversation (lines 262–76)? One actress playing Cordelia said:

> You could so easily do it in a nasty, cynical way – in fact, that is how it is usually done. But in this production, it is just saying: 'I understand why you have behaved as you have, and I don't blame you. Here's a warning, but it is not a cynical warning.' Nevertheless, Regan and Gonerill resented my interference, and spoke their replies sarcastically. Gonerill's line 273, with its use of alliteration (repeated initial letter sound), especially lends itself to sarcasm.

Take parts and speak lines 262–76 to find your own interpretation of the mood in which the sisters say farewell.

2 Princesses in private (in groups of four)

Use lines 277–98 to work on one or both of the following:

a Talk together about the advice a director could give to the actors playing Gonerill and Regan in order to make the differences between their characters as clear as possible.

b Select six different critical comments which Gonerill and Regan make about Lear. When you have made your selection, two group members read aloud Gonerill's lines 50–6 and Regan's lines 64–71. The other two group members interject with the critical comments, so that the sisters' truthful thoughts are heard as well as their insincere public voices.

---

professèd bosoms publicly stated love
At fortune's alms as a gift of charity
scanted stinted, withheld
well are worth ... wanted deserve to be valued as nothing

plighted hidden
long-engraffed long ingrained
choleric ill-tempered
unconstant starts unpredictable behaviour
i'th'heat immediately

CORDELIA The jewels of our father, with washed eyes
    Cordelia leaves you. I know you what you are,
    And like a sister am most loath to call
    Your faults as they are named. Love well our father: 265
    To your professèd bosoms I commit him.
    But yet, alas, stood I within his grace,
    I would prefer him to a better place.
    So farewell to you both.
REGAN Prescribe not us our duty.
GONERILL   Let your study   270
    Be to content your lord, who hath received you
    At fortune's alms. You have obedience scanted,
    And well are worth the want that you have wanted.
CORDELIA Time shall unfold what plighted cunning hides;
    Who covers faults, at last with shame derides.   275
    Well may you prosper.
FRANCE   Come, my fair Cordelia.
                      Exeunt France and Cordelia
GONERILL Sister, it is not little I have to say of what most nearly
    appertains to us both. I think our father will hence tonight.
REGAN That's most certain, and with you; next month with us.
GONERILL You see how full of changes his age is; the observation   280
    we have made of it hath not been little. He always loved our
    sister most, and with what poor judgement he hath now cast
    her off appears too grossly.
REGAN 'Tis the infirmity of his age; yet he hath ever but slenderly
    known himself.   285
GONERILL The best and soundest of his time hath been but rash;
    then must we look from his age to receive not alone the
    imperfections of long-engraffed condition, but therewithal the
    unruly waywardness that infirm and choleric years bring with
    them.   290
REGAN Such unconstant starts are we like to have from him as this
    of Kent's banishment.
GONERILL There is further compliment of leave-taking between
    France and him. Pray you, let us sit together. If our father carry
    authority with such disposition as he bears, this last surrender   295
    of his will but offend us.
REGAN We shall further think of it.
GONERILL We must do something, and i'th'heat.   *Exeunt*

Edmond questions why he is regarded as inferior because his parents were not married. He has a plot to replace his brother, Edgar, as his father's heir. Gloucester expresses concern about events at court.

1 Edmond alone (in groups of four or five)

Lines 1–22 are a soliloquy, a speech by an actor alone on stage. The dramatic convention is that a soliloquy expresses what the character really thinks and feels. An actor can choose whether to address the audience directly, or to speak as if the audience overhears him or her thinking aloud.

Edmond complains about his treatment as a 'bastard' or illegitimate child. Today there is no stigma attached to children born outside marriage, but in Shakespeare's day they were regarded as socially unacceptable, especially among the nobility. Edmond decides to take Nature as his deity or 'goddess', rejecting the social customs which condemn him as inferior. Explore Edmond's soliloquy through one or more of the following:

a Experiment on your own with different ways of speaking the lines.

b Share a group reading, taking turns to speak the words. For instance, by changing readers at each punctuation mark or after each sentence.

c Make a list of Edmond's grievances. Compare the Edmond of these lines with the almost silent character you saw at the start of Act 1 Scene 1.

d Talk together about the impression of Edmond you gain from the soliloquy. Suggest four or five adjectives to describe his character.

e Make up three sixty-second dramas showing different incidents from Edmond's life which may have made him feel inferior to others because of his illegitimacy.

---

in the plague of custom
  condemned by the rules of society
curiosity of nations nit-picking
  laws
Lag of younger than
compact proportioned
issue child

composition bodily perfection
fops fools
speed succeed
Prescribed reduced
Confined to exhibition restricted
  to a small allowance
Upon the gad in haste

ACT I   SCENE 2
The Earl of Gloucester's Castle

Enter EDMOND

EDMOND Thou, Nature, art my goddess; to thy law
    My services are bound. Wherefore should I
    Stand in the plague of custom and permit
    The curiosity of nations to deprive me?
    For that I am some twelve or fourteen moonshines   5
    Lag of a brother? Why 'bastard'? Wherefore 'base'?
    When my dimensions are as well compact,
    My mind as generous, and my shape as true
    As honest madam's issue? Why brand they us
    With 'base'? with 'baseness'? 'bastardy'? 'base, base'?   10
    Who in the lusty stealth of nature take
    More composition and fierce quality
    Than doth within a dull, stale, tired bed
    Go to th'creating a whole tribe of fops
    Got 'tween a sleep and wake? Well then,   15
    Legitimate Edgar, I must have your land.
    Our father's love is to the bastard, Edmond,
    As to th'legitimate. Fine word, 'legitimate'.
    Well, my legitimate, [*Takes out a letter*] if this letter speed
    And my invention thrive, Edmond the base   20
    Shall to th'legitimate. I grow; I prosper;
    Now gods, stand up for bastards!

Enter GLOUCESTER

GLOUCESTER Kent banished thus? and France in choler parted?
    And the king gone tonight? Prescribed his power,
    Confined to exhibition? All this done   25
    Upon the gad? Edmond, how now? What news?

Edmond tricks Gloucester into reading a letter which he claims is from Edgar. The letter suggests that Edgar is seeking his father's death in order to inherit his wealth. Edmond lies about the origin of the letter.

1 'Nothing' – another echo

Once again, the word that will echo through much of the play is heard: 'nothing'. In lines 31–5, it is used by a son and his father. Suggest possible reasons why Shakespeare decided to have the word repeated three times at this point in the play. You will find later that Gloucester's line, 'If it be nothing, I shall not need spectacles', is heavily ironic.

2 The fake letter (in pairs)

This encounter between Edmond and Gloucester echoes the tensions and deceit in Lear's family. It introduces a sub-plot which complements the main story-line of father–child betrayal.

Use the letter as a prop (stage property). Begin with Gloucester's 'What news?', and act out lines 26–44, using a piece of paper as the letter. Add gestures and movements to emphasise the sinister game of cat and mouse as Edmond traps his father.

3 Gloucester's questions (in pairs)

Gloucester's language is full of questions, which may be evidence of a troubled and uncertain mind. One person speaks all the questions Gloucester asks in lines 23–58, pausing after each question. In the pause, the other replies as a member of the audience who has watched the play so far.

---

terrible dispatch sudden concealment
perused read
o'erlooking attention
essay ... virtue test of my good nature
idle ... bondage useless and foolish slavery

who sways ... suffered who rules only because we tolerate it
casement window
closet private room
character handwriting
durst would, dare
fain rather

EDMOND So please your lordship, none. [*Putting up the letter*]
GLOUCESTER Why so earnestly seek you to put up that letter?
EDMOND I know no news, my lord.
GLOUCESTER What paper were you reading?   30
EDMOND Nothing, my lord.
GLOUCESTER No? What needed then that terrible dispatch of it
   into your pocket? The quality of nothing hath not such need to
   hide itself. Let's see. Come, if it be nothing, I shall not need
   spectacles.   35
EDMOND I beseech you, sir, pardon me; it is a letter from my
   brother that I have not all o'erread; and for so much as I have
   perused, I find it not fit for your o'erlooking.
GLOUCESTER Give me the letter, sir.
EDMOND I shall offend either to detain or give it. The contents, as   40
   in part I understand them, are too blame.
GLOUCESTER Let's see, let's see.
EDMOND I hope for my brother's justification he wrote this but as
   an essay or taste of my virtue.
                              [*Gives him the letter*]
GLOUCESTER *Reads* 'This policy and reverence of age makes the   45
   world bitter to the best of our times, keeps our fortunes from us
   till our oldness cannot relish them. I begin to find an idle and
   fond bondage in the oppression of aged tyranny, who sways not
   as it hath power but as it is suffered. Come to me, that of this I
   may speak more. If our father would sleep till I waked him, you   50
   should enjoy half his revenue forever and live the beloved of
   your brother. Edgar.' Hum! Conspiracy! 'Sleep till I waked
   him, you should enjoy half his revenue.' My son Edgar, had he
   a hand to write this? a heart and brain to breed it in? When
   came you to this? Who brought it?   55
EDMOND It was not brought me, my lord; there's the cunning of it.
   I found it thrown in at the casement of my closet.
GLOUCESTER You know the character to be your brother's?
EDMOND If the matter were good, my lord, I durst swear it were
   his: but in respect of that, I would fain think it were not.   60

Gloucester curses Edgar, but Edmond develops the deception further by protesting that his brother cannot be a villain and by advising caution. Edmond proposes to talk to Edgar where their father can overhear them.

1 The language of deceit (in pairs)

Try one or more of the following activities to explore the way in which Edmond uses language cunningly in order to manipulate his father's feelings.

a Identify several lies which Edmond tells his father.

b Find three words or phrases of Edmond's which are probably intended to enrage his father. Find three or four other words and phrases which he uses to suggest his own honesty and loyalty.

c Compare Edmond's deceitful language in lines 62–90 with his soliloquy (lines 1–22), in which he states what he really thinks. Identify three or four examples to show the differences of style and content between his honest and dishonest language.

2 Edmond and the audience

Edmond can be compared to the Vice or Machiavel in medieval plays – a comic but evil figure who often speaks confidentially to the audience, treating them almost as fellow conspirators in his villainous plotting. Work through Edmond's lines opposite, suggesting where he could make movements and gestures to remind the audience of his true intentions. If you think it would be inappropriate for Edmond to be played in this way, give one or two reasons for your decision.

---

sounded you in asked your opinion about

at perfect age adult

testimony ... intent information about his intentions

should ... course won't go wrong

pawn down bet

meet appropriate

an auricular assurance the evidence of your own ears

wind me into him craftily discover his thoughts

I would ... resolution I would give everything to find out the truth

GLOUCESTER It is his.

EDMOND It is his hand, my lord, but I hope his heart is not in the
contents.

GLOUCESTER Has he never before sounded you in this business?

EDMOND Never, my lord. But I have heard him oft maintain it to   65
be fit that, sons at perfect age, and fathers declined, the father
should be as ward to the son, and the son manage his revenue.

GLOUCESTER O villain, villain – his very opinion in the letter!
Abhorred villain, unnatural, detested, brutish villain – worse
than brutish! Go, sirrah, seek him: I'll apprehend him.   70
Abominable villain, where is he?

EDMOND I do not well know, my lord. If it shall please you to
suspend your indignation against my brother till you can derive
from him better testimony of his intent, you should run a
certain course; where if you violently proceed against him,   75
mistaking his purpose, it would make a great gap in your own
honour and shake in pieces the heart of his obedience. I dare
pawn down my life for him that he hath writ this to feel my
affection to your honour and to no other pretence of danger.

GLOUCESTER Think you so?   80

EDMOND If your honour judge it meet, I will place you where you
shall hear us confer of this and by an auricular assurance have
your satisfaction, and that without any further delay than this
very evening.

GLOUCESTER He cannot be such a monster. Edmond, seek him   85
out: wind me into him, I pray you. Frame the business after
your own wisdom. I would unstate myself to be in a due
resolution.

EDMOND I will seek him, sir, presently, convey the business as I
shall find means, and acquaint you withal.   90

Gloucester sees Edgar's treachery as part of a breakdown in society foretold by recent eclipses of the sun and moon. Edmond rejects such superstitious belief in astrology, the influence of the stars on human affairs.

1 An old man fears for his country

Like many older people, Gloucester thinks that society is in decay. He is disturbed by recent eclipses which he thinks foretell the discordant state of Lear's Britain. The eclipses may be understood by 'the wisdom of nature', but their effects are still painful. He catalogues what he sees as unnatural disasters, from the decline of love to the rise of conspiracies ('Machinations') and insincerity ('hollowness'). Work through Gloucester's list of disasters in lines 94–100, and see how many you can match with events in the play.

2 Edmond – realist and schemer (in pairs)

Edmond sceptically observes that, out of convenience, people choose to blame the stars ('heavenly compulsion' and 'spherical predominance') for their personalities. He says that he would have been wicked whichever star sign he was born under. He is what Nature made him!

Edgar's arrival is Edmond's cue to start the second part of his plot to inherit his father's wealth and status. His theatrical language emphasises the fact that he is about to act out a role ('the catastrophe of the old comedy' is the abrupt ending of an old-fashioned play). He ensures that Edgar overhears words which mockingly imitate Gloucester's line 91, and he probably sings 'Fa, sol, la, me', known to Elizabethans as 'the devil in music'.

Experiment with different ideas of what Edmond is doing (or pretending to do) when Edgar enters. What stage business could an actor add to make Edmond seem even more two-faced?

---

sequent following
surfeits excesses
treachers traitors
whoremaster lecherous
to lay ... star to blame his lechery on the stars
compounded had sex with

Dragon's tail conjunction of the waning moon with the sun's orbit (thought to be an evil influence)
Ursa major star cluster (Great Bear)
Tom o'Bedlam madman (see page 74)

GLOUCESTER These late eclipses in the sun and moon portend no
good to us. Though the wisdom of nature can reason it thus
and thus, yet nature finds itself scourged by the sequent effects.
Love cools, friendship falls off, brothers divide. In cities,
mutinies; in countries, discord; in palaces, treason; and the   95
bond cracked 'twixt son and father. This villain of mine comes
under the prediction: there's son against father. The king falls
from bias of nature, there's father against child. We have seen
the best of our time. Machinations, hollowness, treachery, and
all ruinous disorders follow us disquietly to our graves. Find   100
out this villain, Edmond, it shall lose thee nothing. Do it
carefully. And the noble and true-hearted Kent banished; his
offence, honesty. 'Tis strange.   *Exit*
EDMOND This is the excellent foppery of the world, that when we
are sick in fortune, often the surfeits of our own behaviour, we   105
make guilty of our disasters the sun, the moon, and stars; as if
we were villains on necessity, fools by heavenly compulsion,
knaves, thieves, and treachers by spherical predominance,
drunkards, liars, and adulterers by an enforced obedience of
planetary influence; and all that we are evil in, by a divine   110
thrusting on. An admirable evasion of whoremaster man, to lay
his goatish disposition on the charge of a star! My father
compounded with my mother under the Dragon's tail, and my
nativity was under *Ursa major*, so that it follows, I am rough and
lecherous. I should have been that I am had the maidenliest   115
star in the firmament twinkled on my bastardising.

Enter EDGAR

Pat: he comes, like the catastrophe of the old comedy. My cue
is villainous melancholy, with a sigh like Tom o'Bedlam. – O
these eclipses do portend these divisions. Fa, sol, la, me.
EDGAR How now, brother Edmond, what serious contemplation   120
are you in?

Edmond hints that Gloucester has turned against Edgar, who is now in great danger. Edmond tells Edgar to hide, saying that he is on his side. Alone on stage, Edmond looks forward to succeeding by trickery.

1 Edmond the persuader (in pairs)

Just as he tricked his father, Edmond deceives his brother with great ease. He pretends that he wants to protect Edgar from their father's wrath by hiding him at his 'lodging'. In many productions, Edmond speaks very quickly, and even physically takes hold of his brother.

Share a reading of lines 120–50. Afterwards, identify the ways in which Edmond uses cunning to persuade Edgar that he is in danger.

2 Two soliloquies

Scene 2 begins and ends with soliloquies by Edmond. Identify similarities and differences in the two soliloquies. In particular, make clear the different use of the word 'nature' in each one.

3 Additional dialogue – additional insight?

The quarto version of the play (see page 232) includes six extra lines after 'unhappily' in line 126. What could these additional lines suggest about the personalities of Edmond and Edgar?

> as of unnaturalness between the child and the parent, death, dearth, disso-
> lutions of ancient amities, divisions in state, menaces and maledictions against
> king and nobles, needless diffidences, banishment of friends, dissipation of
> cohorts, nuptial breaches, and I know not what.
> EDGAR How long have you been a sectary astronomical?
> EDMOND Come, come,

(To help you: 'diffidences' = doubts, 'dissipation of cohorts' = disbanding armies, 'sectary astronomical' = believer in astrology.)

---

countenance looks
forbear avoid
with the mischief … allay hurting you would barely reduce his anger
have … forbearance keep a low profile, keep your head down

stir abroad go out
anon soon
credulous naïve, unsuspecting
wit cunning
fashion fit use to my own purpose

EDMOND I am thinking, brother, of a prediction I read this other
    day, what should follow these eclipses.

EDGAR Do you busy yourself with that?

EDMOND I promise you, the effects he writes of succeed un-   125
    happily. When saw you my father last?

EDGAR The night gone by.

EDMOND Spake you with him?

EDGAR Ay, two hours together.

EDMOND Parted you in good terms? Found you no displeasure in   130
    him by word nor countenance?

EDGAR None at all.

EDMOND Bethink yourself wherein you may have offended him,
    and at my entreaty forbear his presence until some little time
    hath qualified the heat of his displeasure, which at this instant   135
    so rageth in him that with the mischief of your person it would
    scarcely allay.

EDGAR Some villain hath done me wrong.

EDMOND That's my fear. I pray you have a continent forbearance
    till the speed of his rage goes slower; and as I say, retire with   140
    me to my lodging, from whence I will fitly bring you to hear my
    lord speak. Pray ye, go; there's my key. If you do stir abroad, go
    armed.

EDGAR Armed, brother?

EDMOND Brother, I advise you to the best. I am no honest man, if   145
    there be any good meaning toward you. I have told you what I
    have seen and heard – but faintly, nothing like the image and
    horror of it. Pray you, away.

EDGAR Shall I hear from you anon?

EDMOND I do serve you in this business.   150

                                        Exit [Edgar]

        A credulous father and a brother noble,
        Whose nature is so far from doing harms
        That he suspects none; on whose foolish honesty
        My practices ride easy. I see the business.
        Let me, if not by birth, have lands by wit.   155
        All with me's meet that I can fashion fit.   *Exit*

*Gonerill complains about the unreasonable and unruly behaviour of her
father and his knights. She instructs Oswald that he and the other servants
should show Lear little courtesy and respect.*

1 'One gross crime or other'

Some time has elapsed since Gonerill was last seen with her sister,
Regan, in Scene 1. Lear has put his plan into effect, and has been stay-
ing with Gonerill, to her increasing annoyance and dismay. Gonerill is
tired of her household being disturbed by the disorderly behaviour of
Lear and his one hundred knights. But what exactly have Lear and his
followers done? Write a few lines for Oswald to follow line 3, in which
he gives actual examples of their riotous behaviour.

2 A short scene

Scene 3 is only twenty-two lines long. Imagine that a director decides to
cut it from a production, and that you disagree with that decision. Make
a list of reasons in favour of its inclusion, justifying its dramatic function in such matters as story, character and themes. Then decide
whether or not you would also argue for the inclusion of the following
additional lines which the quarto (see page 232) gives to Gonerill after
line 16:

> Not to be overruled. Idle old man,
> That still would manage those authorities
> That he hath given away! Now, by my life,
> Old fools are babes again, and must be used
> With checks as flatteries when they are seen abused.

---

chiding scolding, telling off
upbraids criticises
trifle trivial matter
come slack of former services
  become less courteous and helpful
  than before

Horns within sound of hunting
  horns
come to question made an issue
distaste dislike
hold my course follow my lead

ACT 1 SCENE 3
The castle of Albany and Gonerill

Enter GONERILL *and her steward* OSWALD

GONERILL Did my father strike my gentleman for chiding of his
    fool?

OSWALD Ay, madam.

GONERILL By day and night, he wrongs me; every hour
    He flashes into one gross crime or other   5
    That sets us all at odds. I'll not endure it.
    His knights grow riotous, and himself upbraids us
    On every trifle. When he returns from hunting,
    I will not speak with him. Say I am sick.
    If you come slack of former services,   10
    You shall do well; the fault of it I'll answer.
              [Horns within]

OSWALD He's coming, madam, I hear him.

GONERILL Put on what weary negligence you please,
    You and your fellows: I'd have it come to question.
    If he distaste it, let him to my sister,   15
    Whose mind and mine I know in that are one.
    Remember what I have said.

OSWALD Well, madam.

GONERILL And let his knights have colder looks among you:
    What grows of it no matter. Advise your fellows so.   20
    I'll write straight to my sister to hold my course.
    Prepare for dinner.
                       Exeunt

Kent hopes that his disguise as a poor man will enable him to re-enter Lear's service. In response to Lear's questions, Kent declares his wish to serve the king.

1 Kent's disguise (in pairs)

Kent is about to take on the role of Caius (a name mentioned only once in the script, in Act 5 Scene 3, line 257), a serving man who wishes to be employed by Lear. Kent hopes that he can disguise his voice as well as his appearance in order to serve his beloved master. In many productions, Kent adopts a rustic, West Country dialect, but many choices are open to the actor. Try one or more of the following:

a Decide which dialect Kent should speak, giving reasons for your choice.

b Design costumes for Kent as a nobleman and as the poor man, Caius.

c Kent has to convince Lear that he is worth employing as a servant. Act out lines 9–38, identifying the ways in which Kent succeeds in persuading Lear that he would be loyal and valuable.

2 Contrasting attitudes

Scene 2 began with Edmond's soliloquy declaring his resolve to be selfish. Kent's lines 1–17 are about serving or respecting others. Choose one or two phrases from each character's lines which reflect their differing beliefs.

3 'Authority'

Line 27 is often a dramatic moment in the theatre. Advise Kent how to speak the single word 'Authority', and advise Lear how to react to it.

---

defuse disguise
intent intention
issue consequence
razed my likeness disguised my appearance
full of labours a hard worker

stay a jot wait a moment
What dost thou profess? what's your job?
countenance bearing, face
fain willingly

ACT 1   SCENE 4
The Great Hall of the castle of Albany and Gonerill

Enter KENT *(disguised)*

KENT If but as well I other accents borrow
That can my speech defuse, my good intent
May carry through itself to that full issue
For which I razed my likeness. Now, banished Kent,
If thou canst serve where thou dost stand condemned,   5
So may it come thy master, whom thou lov'st,
Shall find thee full of labours.

Horns within. Enter LEAR, *[Knights,] and Attendants*

LEAR Let me not stay a jot for dinner. Go, get it ready.
                                           [Exit an Attendant]
How now, what art thou?
KENT A man, sir.   10
LEAR What dost thou profess? What wouldst thou with us?
KENT I do profess to be no less than I seem, to serve him truly that
will put me in trust, to love him that is honest, to converse with
him that is wise and says little, to fear judgement, to fight when
I cannot choose, and to eat no fish.   15
LEAR What art thou?
KENT A very honest-hearted fellow, and as poor as the king.
LEAR If thou be'st as poor for a subject as he's for a king, thou art
poor enough. What wouldst thou?
KENT Service.   20
LEAR Who wouldst thou serve?
KENT You.
LEAR Dost thou know me, fellow?
KENT No, sir; but you have that in your countenance, which I
would fain call master.   25
LEAR What's that?
KENT Authority.
LEAR What services canst thou do?

33

Lear employs Kent. Oswald ignores Lear's command. The knight comments on the disrespect being shown to the king at Gonerill's castle. Lear says that he, too, has noticed the lack of courtesy.

1 Kent's qualities

Kent gives a witty description of his qualities and of the services he can perform (lines 29–35). Invent a gesture for Kent to make to accompany each characteristic. For example, as he says 'I can keep honest counsel', he could tap the side of his nose to show that he can keep a secret. Afterwards, identify two of the qualities which, from your impression of Kent so far, most accurately reflect his personality.

2 Enter (and exit) Oswald

Oswald has been told by Gonerill to adopt a 'weary negligence' towards Lear. Suggest ways in which Oswald could behave in order to antagonise Lear.

3 'Call the clotpoll back' (in pairs)

Lear sends the knight after Oswald to bring him back to give an explanation for his rudeness. The knight returns, reporting that Oswald has flatly and insolently refused the king's command. Improvise the off-stage conversation between the knight and Oswald.

---

keep honest counsel keep a secret
mar spoil
diligence never failing
  industriousness
clotpoll idiot, blockhead
roundest most direct
wont used to

abatement reduction
the general dependants all the
  servants
conception perception, impression
very pretence and purpose
  deliberate act

KENT I can keep honest counsel, ride, run, mar a curious tale in
telling it, and deliver a plain message bluntly. That which   30
ordinary men are fit for, I am qualified in, and the best of me is
diligence.

LEAR How old art thou?

KENT Not so young, sir, to love a woman for singing, nor so old to
dote on her for anything. I have years on my back forty-eight.   35

LEAR Follow me; thou shalt serve me, if I like thee no worse after
dinner. I will not part from thee yet. Dinner, ho, dinner!
Where's my knave? my fool? Go you and call my fool hither.

[Exit an Attendant]

Enter OSWALD

You, you sirrah, where's my daughter?

OSWALD So please you –   *Exit*   40

LEAR What says the fellow there? Call the clotpoll back.

[Exit a Knight]

Where's my fool? Ho, I think the world's asleep.

[Enter KNIGHT]

How now? Where's that mongrel?

KNIGHT He says, my lord, your daughter is not well.

LEAR Why came not the slave back to me when I called him?   45

KNIGHT Sir, he answered me in the roundest manner, he would
not.

LEAR He would not?

KNIGHT My lord, I know not what the matter is, but to my
judgement your highness is not entertained with that cer-   50
emonious affection as you were wont. There's a great abatement of kindness appears as well in the general dependants as
in the duke himself also, and your daughter.

LEAR Ha? Sayest thou so?

KNIGHT I beseech you pardon me, my lord, if I be mistaken, for   55
my duty cannot be silent when I think your highness wronged.

LEAR Thou but rememberest me of mine own conception. I have
perceived a most faint neglect of late, which I have rather
blamed as mine own jealous curiosity than as a very pretence
and purpose of unkindness. I will look further into't. But   60
where's my fool? I have not seen him these two days.

KNIGHT Since my young lady's going into France, sir, the fool
hath much pined away.

Lear strikes Oswald for his rudeness. Kent joins in the assault. The Fool warns Kent about the dangers of following a king who shows such lack of wisdom in dealing with his daughters.

1 'Who am I, sir?' (in small groups)

Ironically, Lear's question raises doubts about his own identity. He is no longer the all-powerful king that he was at the start of the play, and he is beginning to be aware of his changed status.

a One student reads aloud Lear's lines 57–61. Talk together about whether you think that Lear is showing signs of softening and self-doubt.

b Suggest three or four replies which Lear might expect in response to his question, 'Who am I, sir?' (line 67).

c Why do you think Oswald's plain-spoken reply (line 68) angers Lear so much?

d Invent three or four alternative insults which Oswald could use in response to Lear instead of his deliberately disrespectful 'My lady's father'.

2 Tennis and football

Shakespeare's language makes reference to sports which were popular in his time. 'Bandy' (line 72) comes from tennis, and means to hit a ball backwards and forwards. Kent's line 74 suggests that football was at that time considered a low-grade sport, unsuitable for gentlemen. Use this information to work out what you think Kent means by 'I'll teach you differences' (line 76).

cur worthless dog
base lower-class, inferior
lubber clumsy oaf
tarry stay
earnest payment

coxcomb fool's cap
thou … shortly if you cannot flatter, you'll be out of a job
nuncle my uncle (a typical jester's address to his master)

LEAR No more of that, I have noted it well. Go you and tell my
    daughter I would speak with her. 65

[Exit an Attendant]

    Go you, call hither my fool.

[Exit an Attendant]

Enter OSWALD

    Oh, you, sir, you, come you hither, sir, who am I, sir?

OSWALD My lady's father.

LEAR 'My lady's father'? My lord's knave, you whoreson dog, you
    slave, you cur! 70

OSWALD I am none of these, my lord, I beseech your pardon.

LEAR Do you bandy looks with me, you rascal?

[Strikes him]

OSWALD I'll not be strucken, my lord.

KENT *[Tripping him]* Nor tripped neither, you base football player.

LEAR I thank thee, fellow. Thou serv'st me, and I'll love thee. 75

KENT Come, sir, arise, away, I'll teach you differences. Away,
    away. If you will measure your lubber's length again, tarry; but
    away, go to! Have you wisdom?

[Pushes Oswald out]

    So.

LEAR Now, my friendly knave, I thank thee; there's earnest of thy 80
    service.

[Gives Kent money]

Enter FOOL

FOOL Let me hire him, too; here's my coxcomb.

[Offers Kent his cap]

LEAR How now, my pretty knave, how dost thou?

FOOL *[To Kent]* Sirrah, you were best take my coxcomb.

LEAR Why, my boy? 85

FOOL Why? For taking one's part that's out of favour. *[To Kent]*
    Nay, and thou canst not smile as the wind sits, thou'lt catch
    cold shortly. There, take my coxcomb; why, this fellow has
    banished two on's daughters and did the third a blessing
    against his will; if thou follow him, thou must needs wear my 90
    coxcomb. How now, nuncle? Would I had two coxcombs and
    two daughters.

In spite of Lear's threat of a whipping, the Fool continues to be critical of him. In a series of jokes and rhymes, the Fool chides Lear for disowning Cordelia and giving away his kingdom.

1 Hurtful truths in the Fool's humour (in pairs)

a One person speaks lines 82–98. The other interrupts saying either 'Cordelia' or 'Gonerill and Regan' each time the Fool seems to refer to them.

b How could the Fool taunt Lear with 'nothing' in lines 114–16?

c The quarto (see page 232) includes extra dialogue after line 119. If you were putting on a production of the play, would you choose to include these lines?

FOOL Dost thou know the difference, my boy, between a bitter fool and a sweet one?

LEAR No, lad; teach me.

FOOL   That lord that counselled thee
                                To give away thy land,
                        Come place him here by me,
                                Do thou for him stand;
                        The sweet and bitter fool
                                Will presently appear,
                        The one in motley here,
                                The other found out there.

LEAR Dost thou call me fool, boy?

FOOL All thy other titles thou hast given away; that thou wast born with.

KENT This is not altogether fool, my lord.

FOOL No, faith; lords and great men will not let me. If I had a monopoly out, they would have part on't; and ladies too – they will not let me have all the fool to myself; they'll be snatching.

Lady Brach flattering bitch
owest own
goest walk
Learn … trowest don't believe all you hear
Set … throwest don't gamble all you possess

unfeed unpaid
meat yolk
clovest divided
thou bor'st … dirt you were like the old man in the fable who foolishly carried his donkey on his back, trying to be kind

LEAR Why, my boy?

FOOL If I gave them all my living, I'd keep my coxcombs myself. There's mine; beg another of thy daughters.   95

LEAR Take heed, sirrah, the whip.

FOOL Truth's a dog must to kennel. He must be whipped out, when the Lady Brach may stand by th'fire and stink.

LEAR A pestilent gall to me.

FOOL Sirrah, I'll teach thee a speech.   100

LEAR Do.

FOOL Mark it, nuncle:

> Have more than thou showest,
> Speak less than thou knowest,
> Lend less than thou owest,   105
> Ride more than thou goest,
> Learn more than thou trowest,
> Set less than thou throwest,
> Leave thy drink and thy whore,
> And keep in-a-door,   110
> And thou shalt have more,
> Than two tens to a score.

KENT This is nothing, fool.

FOOL Then 'tis like the breath of an unfeed lawyer; you gave me nothing for't. Can you make no use of nothing, nuncle?   115

LEAR Why, no, boy; nothing can be made out of nothing.

FOOL [To Kent] Prithee, tell him so much the rent of his land comes to; he will not believe a fool.

LEAR A bitter fool.

FOOL Nuncle, give me an egg, and I'll give thee two crowns.   120

LEAR What two crowns shall they be?

FOOL Why, after I have cut the egg i'th'middle and eat up the meat, the two crowns of the egg. When thou clovest thy crown i'th'middle and gav'st away both parts, thou bor'st thine ass on thy back o'er the dirt. Thou hadst little wit in thy bald crown   125 when thou gav'st thy golden one away. If I speak like myself in this, let him be whipped that first finds it so.

> [Sings]   Fools had ne'er less grace in a year,
> For wise men are grown foppish,
> And know not how their wits to wear,   130
> Their manners are so apish.

LEAR When were you wont to be so full of songs, sirrah?

The Fool marvels at the contrasting treatment he receives from Lear and from Lear's daughters. Lear reproaches Gonerill for her sour expression. Gonerill criticises Lear's attendants for their loutish behaviour.

1 Lear's story: a world turned upside-down

One of the Fool's verbal tricks is to turn familiar order upside-down. After his song about wise men becoming foolish, he now claims Lear has become a child and his daughters punishing parents.

The Fool's stinging account (lines 133–9) of the way in which Lear has lost his dignity by exchanging authority with his daughters, contains vivid images. Use the Fool's words as captions for a strip cartoon.

2 Gonerill complains – and threatens (in groups of four)

In lines 160–73, Gonerill mounts an attack on Lear's followers and his inability to control them. She seems to blame her father ('put it on / By your allowance') for encouraging their riotous behaviour, and she hints at drastic measures ('redress', 'censure'). For the good of the state, she will take steps to discipline Lear's knights, even if this causes offence and brings shame to her father. The situation will acknowledge the wisdom ('discreet proceeding') of what she intends.

Take parts as Gonerill, Lear, the Fool and Kent. As Gonerill speaks lines 160–73 give her a respectful, quiet hearing. As she reads again, respond more actively. Perhaps her listeners behave like giggling teenagers, or busy themselves with eating or drinking.

---

pared sliced, shaved
O without a figure nothing
Mum, mum hush
He that keeps ... some he who
 gives everything away will
 eventually want some of it back
shelled peascod empty pea-pod

all-licensed unchecked
carp criticise
rank unpleasant, offensive
safe redress sure remedy
put it on encourage it
censure criticism

FOOL I have used it, nuncle, e'er since thou mad'st thy daughters
thy mothers; for when thou gav'st them the rod and put'st down
thine own breeches,   135
[*Sings*]   Then they for sudden joy did weep,
            And I for sorrow sung,
            That such a king should play bo-peep,
            And go the fools among.
Prithee, nuncle, keep a schoolmaster that can teach thy fool to 140
lie. I would fain learn to lie.
LEAR And you lie, sirrah, we'll have you whipped.
FOOL I marvel what kin thou and thy daughters are: they'll have
me whipped for speaking true, thou'lt have me whipped for
lying, and sometimes I am whipped for holding my peace. I had 145
rather be any kind o'thing than a fool, and yet I would not be
thee, nuncle; thou hast pared thy wit o'both sides and left
nothing i'th'middle. Here comes one o'the parings.

Enter GONERILL

LEAR How now, daughter! What makes that frontlet on? You are
too much of late i'th'frown.   150
FOOL Thou wast a pretty fellow when thou hadst no need to care
for her frowning; now thou art an O without a figure. I am
better than thou art now; I am a fool, thou art nothing. [*To
Gonerill*] Yes, forsooth, I will hold my tongue, so your face bids
me, though you say nothing.   155
[*Sings*]   Mum, mum:
            He that keeps nor crust, nor crumb,
            Weary of all, shall want some.
That's a shelled peascod.
GONERILL Not only, sir, this, your all-licensed fool,   160
          But other of your insolent retinue
          Do hourly carp and quarrel, breaking forth
          In rank and not-to-be-endurèd riots. Sir,
          I had thought by making this well known unto you
          To have found a safe redress, but now grow fearful,   165
          By what yourself too late have spoke and done,
          That you protect this course, and put it on
          By your allowance; which if you should, the fault
          Would not 'scape censure, nor the redresses sleep;

Gonerill wishes that Lear would behave wisely. Lear questions both his own identity and Gonerill's. She criticises the debauchery of Lear's followers, and demands that he reduce their number.

1 Cuckoo in the nest?

The Fool follows Gonerill's barely veiled threat to Lear with a proverb (lines 175–6). The cuckoo lays its eggs in other birds' nests and its chicks are aggressive and greedy, pushing out other eggs and taking over. Do you think that the Fool's implied comparison is appropriate?

2 Questions of identity (in groups of three)

Lear seems unable to believe that he is listening to his own daughter ('Are you our daughter?'). Gonerill regrets her father's abandonment of reasonable behaviour ('These dispositions, which of late transport you / From what you rightly are'). The Fool shows regret for Lear's reduced status, speaking of the way in which the natural order of things is being overturned and upset ('the cart draws the horse').

a Write advice for an actor on how to perform Lear's lines 185–9.

b Does Lear behave irresponsibly because of the way in which Gonerill treats him? Talk together about how much a sense of identity and self worth depends on how we are treated by others.

3 The Fool falls silent

The Fool's 'Whoop, / Jug, I love thee!' may just be nonsense, or may echo a popular song of the time. He says nothing further until line 270, much later in this scene. What could he be doing during this time?

---

tender of ... weal care for a healthy state
discreet proceeding sensible action
fraught furnished
dispositions moods
transport you change you
notion understanding

discernings / Are ... lethargied perceptions are dulled
admiration play-acting
deboshed debauched
epicurism gluttony
disquantity your train reduce your followers

Which in the tender of a wholesome weal 170
Might in their working do you that offence
Which else were shame, that then necessity
Will call discreet proceeding.
FOOL For you know, nuncle,
    The hedge-sparrow fed the cuckoo so long, 175
    That it's had it head bit off by it young.
So out went the candle, and we were left darkling.
LEAR Are you our daughter?
GONERILL I would you would make use of your good wisdom,
    Whereof I know you are fraught, and put away 180
    These dispositions, which of late transport you
    From what you rightly are.
FOOL May not an ass know when the cart draws the horse? Whoop,
    Jug, I love thee!
LEAR Does any here know me? This is not Lear: 185
    Does Lear walk thus? speak thus? Where are his eyes?
    Either his notion weakens, his discernings
    Are lethargied – Ha! Waking? 'Tis not so!
    Who is it that can tell me who I am?
FOOL Lear's shadow. 190
LEAR Your name, fair gentlewoman?
GONERILL This admiration, sir, is much o'th'savour
    Of other your new pranks. I do beseech you
    To understand my purposes aright:
    As you are old and reverend, should be wise. 195
    Here do you keep a hundred knights and squires,
    Men so disordered, so deboshed and bold,
    That this our court, infected with their manners,
    Shows like a riotous inn; epicurism and lust
    Makes it more like a tavern or a brothel 200
    Than a graced palace. The shame itself doth speak
    For instant remedy. Be then desired
    By her, that else will take the thing she begs,
    A little to disquantity your train,
    And the remainders that shall still depend 205
    To be such men as may besort your age,
    Which know themselves and you.

Lear furiously declares that he will go to Regan. He attacks Gonerill's ingratitude, and defends his followers' honour. He expresses anguish at his treatment of Cordelia. Puzzled, Albany tries to soothe Lear.

In this Stratford production, the stage erupted at Lear's 'Darkness and devils!'. He kicked over a table, and his knights brawled with Gonerill's servants, breaking up the furniture.

train followers
kite scavenging bird of prey
parts accomplishments
exact regard strict attention to
  detail

The worships ... name their
  honour
engine destructive machine
gall bitterness

LEAR   Darkness and devils!
  Saddle my horses; call my train together. –
  Degenerate bastard, I'll not trouble thee;
  Yet have I left a daughter.   210
GONERILL You strike my people, and your disordered rabble
  Make servants of their betters.

Enter ALBANY

LEAR   Woe that too late repents!
  Is it your will? Speak, sir. Prepare my horses.
  Ingratitude! Thou marble-hearted fiend,
  More hideous when thou show'st thee in a child   215
  Than the sea-monster.
ALBANY Pray, sir, be patient.
LEAR [*To Gonerill*]   Detested kite, thou liest!
  My train are men of choice and rarest parts,
  That all particulars of duty know,
  And in the most exact regard support   220
  The worships of their name. O most small fault,
  How ugly didst thou in Cordelia show!
  Which, like an engine, wrenched my frame of nature
  From the fixed place, drew from my heart all love,
  And added to the gall. O Lear, Lear, Lear!   225
  Beat at this gate that let thy folly in
  And thy dear judgement out. Go, go, my people.
ALBANY My lord, I am guiltless as I am ignorant
  Of what hath moved you.

Lear curses Gonerill with childlessness or unloving children. He leaves, but returns having discovered Gonerill's dismissal of fifty of his followers. Lear weeps and resumes cursing Gonerill, claiming that Regan will welcome him.

1 A father's curse (in pairs)

Lear has already called Gonerill a 'degenerate bastard' (line 209), and now he brings down a curse of childlessness upon her. One person speaks Lear's lines 230–44, while the other plays Gonerill and reacts to all Lear says. Afterwards, talk together about why Lear's language is so hateful in its references to childlessness and filial ingratitude.

2 Lear weeps (in groups of three to four)

In lines 251–65, Lear is reduced to weeping. He is enraged by his own vulnerability, as well as outraged by Gonerill's attitude. Share three group readings to explore each of the following elements: Lear's sense of helplessness, his childishness, and his sensitivity about his manhood.

After your reading, prepare a dramatic presentation of lines 251–65. All group members will represent Lear – divide the words between you as you choose. Add mime, gesture and movement.

3 Kent's version (in pairs)

Kent is only one of many silent or near silent witnesses to the events of this scene. At line 244, Kent leaves with the king, but he has not spoken since Gonerill came on stage. Imagine that, immediately after he leaves, Kent speaks two lines to Lear which he hopes will help the enraged king. Write Kent's two lines.

---

increase reproduction	**fret** wear away
derogate degraded	**a clap** one stroke
teem bear children	**perforce** against my will
spleen malice	**Th'untented woundings** the
thwart disnatured perverse	untreated injuries
unnatural	**temper** soften
cadent falling	

LEAR   It may be so, my lord.
    Hear, Nature, hear, dear goddess, hear: 230
    Suspend thy purpose, if thou didst intend
    To make this creature fruitful.
    Into her womb convey sterility,
    Dry up in her the organs of increase,
    And from her derogate body never spring   235
    A babe to honour her. If she must teem,
    Create her child of spleen, that it may live
    And be a thwart disnatured torment to her.
    Let it stamp wrinkles in her brow of youth,
    With cadent tears fret channels in her cheeks,   240
    Turn all her mother's pains and benefits
    To laughter and contempt, that she may feel
    How sharper than a serpent's tooth it is
    To have a thankless child. Away, away!
            Exeunt [Lear, Kent, Knights, and Attendants]
ALBANY Now, gods that we adore, whereof comes this?   245
GONERILL Never afflict yourself to know more of it,
    But let his disposition have that scope
    As dotage gives it.

Enter LEAR

LEAR What, fifty of my followers at a clap?
    Within a fortnight?
ALBANY   What's the matter, sir?   250
LEAR I'll tell thee. [*To Gonerill*] Life and death! I am ashamed
    That thou hast power to shake my manhood thus,
    That these hot tears, which break from me perforce,
    Should make thee worth them. Blasts and fogs upon thee!
    Th'untented woundings of a father's curse   255
    Pierce every sense about thee. Old fond eyes,
    Beweep this cause again, I'll pluck ye out
    And cast you with the waters that you loose
    To temper clay. Ha! Let it be so.
    I have another daughter,   260
    Who I am sure is kind and comfortable.
    When she shall hear this of thee, with her nails
    She'll flay thy wolvish visage. Thou shalt find
    That I'll resume the shape which thou dost think
    I have cast off forever.   *Exit*

Gonerill fears the dangers posed by Lear and his knights. She believes that such suspicion is safer than trust, and sends Oswald to warn Regan. Gonerill hints that Albany's gentle nature is a weakness in a ruler.

1 'The Fool follows after'

The Fool's words are often a mixture of sense and nonsense. It is usually inappropriate to analyse them in great detail to try to derive an exact meaning. So, if you can only gain a general sense of what he means in lines 271–5, don't worry. But the actor playing the Fool has to make the language significant to the audience. Suggest how he should deliver his final lines.

2 Once and future king? (in small groups)

In lines 263–5, Lear appears to be threatening to reclaim his former power and to revoke his abdication. Speculate about what might happen to the main characters in the play if Lear were to become ruler of Britain again.

3 Husband and wife relationships (in pairs)

Gonerill interrupts Albany as he talks of his love for her. She speaks to him sarcastically about allowing Lear to keep a hundred knights, then challenges his judgement and strength of character.

a Take parts and speak everything Gonerill and Albany say to one another in lines 265–302. Afterwards, talk together about how you think they really feel about each other.

b How far do you agree with the student who said: 'The total difference between them, and between their outlooks, is summed up in what they both say in line 282'?

---

partial biased
halter hangman's noose
politic sensible
At point armed and ready
buzz rumour
enguard protect

compact strengthen
This milky gentleness and course
these mild and gentle ways
ataxed blamed
harmful mildness gentleness that
is harmful to the state

GONERILL   Do you mark that?   265
ALBANY I cannot be so partial, Gonerill,
    To the great love I bear you –
GONERILL   Pray you, content.
    What, Oswald, ho!
    You, sir, more knave than fool, after your master.
FOOL Nuncle Lear, nuncle Lear, tarry, take the fool with thee.   270
        A fox, when one has caught her,
        And such a daughter,
        Should sure to the slaughter,
        If my cap would buy a halter;
        So the fool follows after.   *Exit*   275
GONERILL This man hath had good counsel. A hundred knights?
    'Tis politic and safe to let him keep
    At point a hundred knights? Yes, that on every dream,
    Each buzz, each fancy, each complaint, dislike,
    He may enguard his dotage with their powers   280
    And hold our lives in mercy. Oswald, I say!
ALBANY Well, you may fear too far.
GONERILL   Safer than trust too far.
    Let me still take away the harms I fear,
    Not fear still to be taken. I know his heart.
    What he hath uttered I have writ my sister: 285
    If she sustain him and his hundred knights
    When I have showed th'unfitness –

             Enter OSWALD

               How now, Oswald?
    What, have you writ that letter to my sister?
OSWALD Ay, madam.
GONERILL Take you some company and away to horse.   290
    Inform her full of my particular fear,
    And thereto add such reasons of your own
    As may compact it more. Get you gone,
    And hasten your return.
                  [*Exit Oswald*]
           No, no, my lord,
    This milky gentleness and course of yours,   295
    Though I condemn not, yet under pardon
    You are much more ataxed for want of wisdom,
    Than praised for harmful mildness.

Albany decides to wait for whatever happens. Lear sends Kent with letters to Regan. The Fool predicts that Regan's treatment of Lear will be the same as Gonerill's. Lear recalls his mistreatment of Cordelia.

1 Instructing messengers

Two messengers and two letters are on their way to Regan. Look back at Gonerill's instructions to Oswald in lines 290–4, and contrast them with the ones her father issues to Kent in lines 1–4. What reasons can you think of for the differences between the instructions?

2 The king and the Fool (in pairs)

The Fool directs a series of barbed jokes at Lear in lines 6–38. Sometimes Lear appears to respond, but at other times he seems to be lost in his own thoughts about Cordelia or about revenge against Gonerill. In one production of the play, the lines were played as though the two characters were a comedy double act. Each 'punchline' was accompanied by appropriate gestures and stamping of feet. In another production, the Fool was barely able to attract Lear's attention.

Take parts and experiment with different styles of performing all the exchanges between Lear and the Fool. Make clear by Lear's tone of voice or body language whether or not he is really listening to the Fool. Think about whether or not you want to emphasise the humour or the pathos of this scene, or about how you could do justice to both.

---

mar make worse
diligence attention to the task
kibes chilblains
thy wit ... slipshod your brain won't need slippers because you don't have a brain

kindly in the same way as her sister
crab a small, sour fruit (crab apple)

ALBANY How far your eyes may pierce I cannot tell;
    Striving to better, oft we mar what's well.   300
GONERILL Nay then –
ALBANY Well, well, th'event.

Exeunt

ACT 1   SCENE 5
Outside the castle of Albany and Gonerill

Enter LEAR, KENT (disguised), and FOOL

LEAR Go you before to Gloucester with these letters. Acquaint my
    daughter no further with anything you know than comes from
    her demand out of the letter. If your diligence be not speedy, I
    shall be there afore you.
KENT I will not sleep, my lord, till I have delivered your letter.   5

Exit

FOOL If a man's brains were in's heels, were't not in danger of
    kibes?
LEAR Ay, boy.
FOOL Then, I prithee, be merry; thy wit shall not go slipshod.
LEAR Ha, ha, ha.   10
FOOL Shalt see thy other daughter will use thee kindly, for though
    she's as like this as a crab's like an apple, yet I can tell what I
    can tell.
LEAR What canst tell, boy?
FOOL She will taste as like this as a crab does to a crab. Thou   15
    canst tell why one's nose stands i'th'middle on's face?
LEAR No.
FOOL Why, to keep one's eyes of either side 's nose, that what a
    man cannot smell out, he may spy into.
LEAR I did her wrong.   20

The Fool continues his barbed jokes, but Lear's mind seems elsewhere, as he thinks of seizing back the kingdom and of Gonerill's ingratitude. Lear fears insanity. As he leaves, the Fool makes a sexual joke.

1 Foolish jokes? (in pairs)

The Fool is playing the traditional role as the king's 'all-licensed fool' (see page 214). He may be trying to cheer up the king, but he is also being very critical of Lear's behaviour, reminding him of the mistakes he has made.

a Work through lines 6–38 and remind each other of the cutting criticism in each of the Fool's jokes or riddles. (Don't spend too much time on this, because the quickest way to kill a joke is to analyse it!)

b Invent and rehearse further jokes at Lear's expense which combine humour with reminders of his unwise behaviour.

2 What's in Lear's mind?

Identify who or what Lear is thinking of at lines 20, 27, 32, and 37–8.

3 Last words

Some critics claim that the Fool's intention in lines 42–3 is to say that his words have a serious meaning. But these lines clearly contain a sexual innuendo. Actors often emphasise the phallic joke with graphic gestures. Decide on possible reasons why Shakespeare chose to end the first act on this sexual note.

case covering
asses fools, servants
mo more

perforce violently
in temper sane
maid virgin

FOOL Canst tell how an oyster makes his shell?

LEAR No.

FOOL Nor I neither; but I can tell why a snail has a house.

LEAR Why?

FOOL Why, to put 's head in, not to give it away to his daughters,   25
    and leave his horns without a case.

LEAR I will forget my nature. So kind a father! Be my horses ready?

FOOL Thy asses are gone about 'em. The reason why the seven
    stars are no mo than seven is a pretty reason.

LEAR Because they are not eight.   30

FOOL Yes, indeed, thou wouldst make a good fool.

LEAR To take't again perforce. Monster ingratitude!

FOOL If thou wert my fool, nuncle, I'd have thee beaten for being
    old before thy time.

LEAR How's that?   35

FOOL Thou shouldst not have been old till thou hadst been wise.

LEAR O let me not be mad, not mad, sweet heaven!
       Keep me in temper, I would not be mad.

[*Enter* GENTLEMAN]

       How now, are the horses ready?

GENTLEMAN Ready, my lord.   40

LEAR Come, boy.

FOOL She that's a maid now, and laughs at my departure,
       Shall not be a maid long, unless things be cut shorter.

Exeunt

Looking back at Act 1
Activities for groups or individuals

1 The entrance of the royal family

The entrance of Lear and his court in Scene 1 can be presented in very different ways. The 1993 RSC production opened in a busy, festive mood, with the courtiers and royal family already on stage, laughing and talking. Other productions have chosen to play the opening scene as a tense political meeting, or as a spectacular ceremonial occasion. Study the list of characters on page 1. Decide the order in which each character will enter, and the way in which their status can be shown. Prepare and act out a performance of Lear's entrance.

2 The map

Line 32 in Scene 1 shows Lear using a map to divide up his kingdom. In one production, the Fool daubed Lear's divisions in red paint on a huge map which filled the floor of the stage. You can see another way of presenting the map in the painting on the cover of this edition. Sketch your ideas of different ways in which the map of Britain could be shown.

3 The bond

Some critics have said that Cordelia is smug and self-righteous in her refusal to participate in the love test. Cordelia loves her father according to her 'bond'. One of the meanings of the word 'bond' is a legal document or contract. Draw up a 'family bond' which states the duties and obligations of a modern father and teenage daughter towards each other.

4 Lear's folly

During Act 1, Kent, Gonerill and the Fool all accuse Lear of grave failures of judgement. Write three short statements in which each character lists and comments on these misjudgements. Try to make the style of each statement appropriate to the character concerned.

5 Different perspectives

Retell the events of Act 1 from each of the following viewpoints:

- as a family drama – the problems of fathers and children
- as a political drama – the struggle for power in a state
- as a feminist interpretation – the story retold from a woman's point of view
- as a fairy story for very young children.

What does this moment from Scene 1 suggest about the relationship between Lear and Cordelia?

Curan informs Edmond of Cornwall and Regan's imminent arrival, and of the growing tension between Cornwall and Albany. Edmond tries to convince the innocent Edgar to flee his father's castle.

1 'Ear-kissing arguments' (in pairs)

Britain is now awash with rumours and gossip about the strange and perplexing events of Act 1. Lear has divided his power and his kingdom between his daughters Regan and Gonerill, and disinherited his youngest and favourite daughter, Cordelia. Kent, one of Lear's trusted and loyal noblemen, has been banished on pain of death.

Act 2 opens with Curan, a courtier, adding to the tense atmosphere of concern and anxiety by telling of the growing rift and 'likely wars' between Cornwall and Albany. Rumours abound of the foolish behaviour of the king, of the bitter struggle for power between his beneficiaries, and of the volatile nature of domestic politics.

Using mime or any other appropriate means, demonstrate what you think Curan means by an 'ear-kissing argument'. Afterwards, talk together about why the expression is so apt in the current political climate.

2 Edmond sets to work (in pairs)

In lines 14–27, Edmond begins his plan to discredit Edgar. He appeals to the personified qualities of Briefness and Fortune to help him quickly seize and use the opportunity. As a result, his lines to Edgar are full of short, sharp statements, commands and questions.

Take parts and read aloud lines 19–32. Bring out the urgency of the way in which Edmond works on, and manipulates Edgar, persuading him to run away.

severally separately
Save thee God save you
pray you please tell me
'twixt between
perforce by chance

queasy question difficult nature
hither here
Upon his party on Cornwall's side
Advise yourself think carefully

ACT 2 SCENE 1

The Great Hall of Gloucester's castle, at night

Enter EDMOND *and* CURAN, *severally*

EDMOND Save thee, Curan.

CURAN And you, sir. I have been with your father and given him
notice that the Duke of Cornwall and Regan his duchess will
be here with him this night.

EDMOND How comes that?   5

CURAN Nay, I know not. You have heard of the news abroad? I
mean the whispered ones, for they are yet but ear-kissing
arguments.

EDMOND Not I; pray you, what are they?

CURAN Have you heard of no likely wars toward 'twixt the Dukes   10
of Cornwall and Albany?

EDMOND Not a word.

CURAN You may do then in time. Fare you well, sir.   *Exit*

EDMOND The duke be here tonight! The better, best.
This weaves itself perforce into my business.   15
My father hath set guard to take my brother,
And I have one thing of a queasy question
Which I must act. Briefness and Fortune, work!
Brother, a word, descend; brother, I say!

Enter EDGAR

My father watches: O sir, fly this place.   20
Intelligence is given where you are hid;
You have now the good advantage of the night.
Have you not spoken 'gainst the Duke of Cornwall?
He's coming hither, now i'th'night, i'th'haste,
And Regan with him. Have you nothing said   25
Upon his party 'gainst the Duke of Albany?
Advise yourself.

EDGAR   I am sure on't, not a word.

*Edmond stages a mock skirmish with Edgar, and deliberately wounds himself.
Edgar flees, and Gloucester sends servants to pursue him. Edmond lies about
Edgar's wicked intentions towards him and his father.*

1 Shouts and whispers

Edmond hears his father coming and quickly devises a plan to stage a
fight with Edgar. Edmond wants to disorient his brother, and heighten
his father's fear and sense of imminent danger.

In lines 28–36, Edmond intends some words to be heard by Edgar
alone, and some by the guards and Gloucester. An actor may even
choose to make Edgar's line 28, 'I hear my father coming', a statement
aimed at Gloucester. Other words Edmond speaks to himself, or perhaps to the audience.

Explore different ways of speaking lines 28–36.

2 Edmond persuades his father (in groups of four)

Edmond sets out to convince his father of Edgar's guilt. He prepares by
shouting for effect, by wounding himself, and by talking of things
which he knows will have an impact on Gloucester. Edmond cunningly
exploits Gloucester's superstitions, and his hatred of the wickedness of
offences committed against fathers. Earlier, Edmond played on
Gloucester's gullibility with the forged letter (Act 1 Scene 2, lines
27–103). Now Edmond continues to stress how 'unnatural' Edgar's
intentions are, going against the natural duties and bonds of family.

Pick out the words or phrases in lines 37–55 which you think will
have a strong effect on Gloucester. As one person speaks the lines, the
others echo the 'key words' to emphasise their significance. Afterwards,
identify which of Edmond's words are true, and which are lies.

---

quit you well fight well
beget … endeavour give the
  impression of my violent struggle
conjuring the moon calling on the
  moon goddess
stand auspicious mistress be his
  guiding goddess

parricides father-killers
bend aim
in fine in conclusion
loathly opposite bitterly opposed
in fell motion with deadly thrust
unprovided unarmed
latched caught

EDMOND I hear my father coming. Pardon me,
    In cunning, I must draw my sword upon you.
    Draw, seem to defend yourself. Now, quit you well.   30
    [*Shouting*] Yield! Come before my father! – Light ho,
      here! –
    Fly, brother! – Torches, torches! – so, farewell.

                                         Exit Edgar

    Some blood drawn on me would beget opinion
    Of my more fierce endeavour.
              [*Wounds his arm*]
                   I have seen drunkards
    Do more than this in sport. Father, father!   35
    Stop, stop! No help?

     Enter GLOUCESTER, *and Servants with torches*

GLOUCESTER   Now, Edmond, where's the villain?
EDMOND Here stood he in the dark, his sharp sword out,
    Mumbling of wicked charms, conjuring the moon
    To stand auspicious mistress.
GLOUCESTER   But where is he?
EDMOND Look, sir, I bleed.
GLOUCESTER   Where is the villain, Edmond?   40
EDMOND Fled this way, sir, when by no means he could –
GLOUCESTER Pursue him, ho! Go after.
                      [*Exeunt Servants*]
               'By no means' what?
EDMOND Persuade me to the murder of your lordship,
    But that I told him the revenging gods
    'Gainst parricides did all the thunder bend,   45
    Spoke with how manifold and strong a bond
    The child was bound to'th'father; sir, in fine,
    Seeing how loathly opposite I stood
    To his unnatural purpose, in fell motion
    With his preparèd sword he charges home   50
    My unprovided body, latched mine arm;
    And when he saw my best alarumed spirits
    Bold in the quarrel's right, roused to th'encounter,
    Or whether ghasted by the noise I made,
    Full suddenly he fled.

Gloucester declares that Edgar must be caught and executed. Edmond continues to lie about Edgar. Convinced of Edgar's villainy, Gloucester plans to reward Edmond with his brother's inheritance.

1 Edmond forces his advantage

Edmond continues to persuade Gloucester of Edgar's villainy by reporting an alleged conversation with his brother. Edmond plays on the prejudice against bastard children, and uses it to his own advantage.

Read aloud lines 66–76 in which Edmond imitates his brother. Try a variety of styles: mocking, sincere, deliberately exaggerated, and so on. Which do you think will work best to persuade Gloucester?

2 Edgar's wanted poster

Gloucester plans to use Cornwall's authority to announce the penalty of death on Edgar, whom he calls a 'murderous coward'. Edgar will be hunted throughout the country.

Design a 'wanted' poster for Edgar. Include his crime, the penalty and the reward. Also incorporate the penalty for anyone who shelters Edgar. Base your ideas on lines 55–62.

3 Two brothers (in groups of three or four)

Gloucester describes Edgar as a 'strange and fastened villain' (unnatural and a confirmed villain), and Edmond as 'loyal and natural'. Suggest other pairs of words to describe Edgar and Edmond. For example, Edgar as 'trusting and naïve' and Edmond as 'plausible and confident'. As you read on, keep these descriptions in mind, and amend or add to them as you discover other aspects of their personalities.

---

dispatch be executed
arch lord
to the stake to the place of
  execution
pight determined
unpossessing land-less
reposal placing

faithed believed
character handwriting
thou ... world you must think
  people stupid
Tucket trumpet call
capable able to inherit

GLOUCESTER   Let him fly far,   55
    Not in this land shall he remain uncaught;
    And found, dispatch. The noble duke my master,
    My worthy arch and patron, comes tonight.
    By his authority I will proclaim it,
    That he which finds him shall deserve our thanks,   60
    Bringing the murderous coward to the stake;
    He that conceals him, death.
EDMOND When I dissuaded him from his intent
    And found him pight to do it, with cursed speech
    I threatened to discover him. He replied,   65
    'Thou unpossessing bastard, dost thou think,
    If I would stand against thee, would the reposal
    Of any trust, virtue, or worth in thee
    Make thy words faithed? No; what I should deny
    (As this I would, ay, though thou didst produce   70
    My very character) I'd turn it all
    To thy suggestion, plot, and damnèd practice;
    And thou must make a dullard of the world,
    If they not thought the profits of my death
    Were very pregnant and potential spirits   75
    To make thee seek it.'
                Tucket within
GLOUCESTER   O strange and fastened villain!
    Would he deny his letter, said he?
    Hark, the duke's trumpets. I know not why he comes.
    All ports I'll bar, the villain shall not 'scape;
    The duke must grant me that. Besides, his picture   80
    I will send far and near, that all the kingdom
    May have due note of him; and of my land,
    Loyal and natural boy, I'll work the means
    To make thee capable.

Regan blames Lear's ill-disciplined knights for encouraging Edgar to murder Gloucester. Cornwall praises Edmond's efforts in thwarting Edgar's plans, and takes Edmond into his service.

1 Different people, different language (in pairs)

What characters say and the way in which they say it often depends upon the status of the person they are addressing. When the Duke of Cornwall arrives, the language of both Gloucester and Edmond seems to undergo a significant change.

Take parts as Edmond and Gloucester and speak lines 63–84, followed by Edmond's lines 96, 105 and 116–17 and Gloucester's lines 89, 92 and 95. Identify the contrasts between the way in which they speak before and after the Duke of Cornwall and Regan enter. Suggest possible reasons why Edmond and Gloucester change their manner of speaking. Do you think that your own language changes as you talk to different people?

2 A letter from Gonerill

In line 98, Regan blames Lear's 'riotous knights' for encouraging Edgar to murder Gloucester. Regan tells of a letter she has received from Gonerill (line 101) giving further details of the unruly behaviour of Lear's one hundred followers. Write the letter.

3 Accurate descriptions? (in groups of three or four)

Cornwall gives a glowing commendation of Edmond. In particular, he praises Edmond's devoted, dutiful service of his father ('child-like office'). He also acknowledges Edmond's 'virtue and obedience', and his possession of a nature 'of deep trust'. However, Cornwall is unaware that his description is heavily ironic. All three of his assessments are inaccurate. Consider each of Cornwall's judgements in turn, and re-write it to express what Edmond is really like.

How dost how are you?
tended upon waited, served
consort company, gang
ill affected disloyal
put him on encouraged him to
  bring about

revenues income
sojourn stay
bewray expose, reveal
strength authority, power, resources

Enter CORNWALL, REGAN, *and Attendants*

CORNWALL How now, my noble friend, since I came hither,   85
    Which I can call but now, I have heard strange news.
REGAN If it be true, all vengeance comes too short
    Which can pursue th'offender. How dost, my lord?
GLOUCESTER O madam, my old heart is cracked, it's cracked.
REGAN What, did my father's godson seek your life?   90
    He whom my father named, your Edgar?
GLOUCESTER O lady, lady, shame would have it hid.
REGAN Was he not companion with the riotous knights
    That tended upon my father?
GLOUCESTER I know not, madam; 'tis too bad, too bad.   95
EDMOND Yes, madam, he was of that consort.
REGAN No marvel, then, though he were ill affected.
    'Tis they have put him on the old man's death,
    To have th'expense and waste of his revenues.
    I have this present evening from my sister   100
    Been well informed of them, and with such cautions,
    That if they come to sojourn at my house,
    I'll not be there.
CORNWALL   Nor I, assure thee, Regan.
    Edmond, I hear that you have shown your father
    A child-like office.
EDMOND   It was my duty, sir.   105
GLOUCESTER He did bewray his practice, and received
    This hurt you see, striving to apprehend him.
CORNWALL Is he pursued?
GLOUCESTER Ay, my good lord.
CORNWALL If he be taken, he shall never more   110
    Be feared of doing harm. Make your own purpose
    How in my strength you please. For you, Edmond,
    Whose virtue and obedience doth this instant
    So much commend itself, you shall be ours;
    Natures of such deep trust we shall much need;   115
    You we first seize on.
EDMOND   I shall serve you, sir,
    Truly, however else.
GLOUCESTER   For him I thank your grace.
CORNWALL You know not why we came to visit you?

Regan speaks of her hazardous night journey. She tells Gloucester that she urgently needs his advice. In Scene 2, Kent, in disguise, picks a quarrel with Oswald by insulting him.

1 'Threading dark-eyed night'

Regan offers a vivid image of the journey to Gloucester's castle (line 119). Suggest how the image conjures up the difficulties experienced by travellers journeying at night in such far-off times.

2 Another letter, another point of view

Regan tells of receiving letters from Lear and Gonerill which express the growing rift ('differences') between father and daughter. Write Lear's letter to Regan in which he offers his version of events.

3 Insulting Oswald (in large groups)

In lines 13–21, Kent mounts a passionate attack on Oswald. His language bristles with energetic and extravagant insults:

'broken meats' – leftovers from a meal
'worsted' – wool worn by servants
'lily-livered' – cowardly
'action-taking' – always going to law
'glass-gazing' – self-admiring, conceited
'superserviceable' – willing to serve in any way
'finical' – fussy
'bawd', 'pander' – pimp

One person plays Oswald (volunteers only!). The other group members stand in a circle around Oswald, and take turns to speak as Kent. Change speaker at each punctuation mark. Repeat the activity with each Kent adding movement and gesture to his insult.

---

prize significance
from our home away from home
attend dispatch are waiting to be sent back
craves ... use demands immediate action

I'th'mire in the bog
Lipsbury pinfold in my grip (pinfold = sheep pen)
addition a mark of rank or importance

REGAN Thus out of season, threading dark-eyed night?
       Occasions, noble Gloucester, of some prize,   120
       Wherein we must have use of your advice.
       Our father he hath writ, so hath our sister,
       Of differences, which I best thought it fit
       To answer from our home. The several messengers
       From hence attend dispatch. Our good old friend,   125
       Lay comforts to your bosom and bestow
       Your needful counsel to our businesses,
       Which craves the instant use.
GLOUCESTER   I serve you, madam;
       Your graces are right welcome.   *Exeunt. Flourish*

ACT 2   SCENE 2
The entrance to Gloucester's castle

Enter KENT (disguised) and OSWALD, *severally*

OSWALD Good dawning to thee, friend. Art of this house?
KENT Ay.
OSWALD Where may we set our horses?
KENT I'th'mire.
OSWALD Prithee, if thou lov'st me, tell me.   5
KENT I love thee not.
OSWALD Why, then I care not for thee.
KENT If I had thee in Lipsbury pinfold, I would make thee care for
    me.
OSWALD Why dost thou use me thus? I know thee not.   10
KENT Fellow, I know thee.
OSWALD What dost thou know me for?
KENT A knave, a rascal, an eater of broken meats, a base, proud,
    shallow, beggarly, three-suited, hundred-pound, filthy worsted-
    stocking knave; a lily-livered, action-taking, whoreson glass-   15
    gazing, superserviceable, finical rogue; one-trunk-inheriting
    slave; one that wouldst be a bawd in way of good service, and
    art nothing but the composition of a knave, beggar, coward,
    pander, and the son and heir of a mongrel bitch, one whom
    I will beat into clamorous whining if thou deniest the least   20
    syllable of thy addition.

Kent insults Oswald again, and draws his sword. Oswald calls for help. Kent threatens Edmond, and Cornwall demands an explanation. Kent further insults Oswald, who seizes the chance to get his own back.

1 Kent versus Oswald (in pairs)

The exchanges between Kent and Oswald are often presented on stage in such a way that their comic aspects are highlighted. But stage-fighting needs a great deal of planning to make it appear spontaneous in performance.

Work out what advice you would give about lines 22–37 to the actors playing Oswald and Kent. In particular, think about:

- how Oswald responds to Kent drawing his sword (line 28)
- how Oswald responds to Kent's threats (lines 30, 35 and 37)
- whether or not Oswald feels in real danger
- when Oswald recognises Kent as the man who previously assaulted him
- why Kent is so keen to fight
- the effect on the combatants of the entrance of Cornwall.

2 'Vanity the puppet'

In line 32, Kent describes Gonerill as 'Vanity the puppet'. Capture the image as a drawing or other illustration.

---

rail on insult
brazen-faced varlet determined rogue
I'll make ... moonshine I'll puncture you full of holes to let in the moonlight
cullionly despicable, servile
barber-monger vain person (spending time at the barber's)

carbonado your shanks slash your legs
goodman boy arrogant young man
disclaims in renounces having any part in
at suit of in pity of

OSWALD Why, what a monstrous fellow art thou, thus to rail on
one that is neither known of thee nor knows thee!

KENT What a brazen-faced varlet art thou to deny thou knowest
me! Is it two days since I tripped up thy heels and beat thee   25
before the king? Draw, you rogue! For though it be night, yet
the moon shines. I'll make a sop o'th'moonshine of you,
[*Drawing his sword*] you whoreson cullionly barber-monger,
draw!

OSWALD Away, I have nothing to do with thee.   30

KENT Draw, you rascal. You come with letters against the king,
and take Vanity the puppet's part against the royalty of her
father. Draw, you rogue, or I'll so carbonado your shanks –
draw, you rascal, come your ways!

OSWALD Help, ho, murder, help!   35

KENT Strike, you slave! Stand, rogue! Stand, you neat slave, strike!

OSWALD Help, ho, murder, murder!

Enter EDMOND, CORNWALL, REGAN, GLOUCESTER, *Servants*

EDMOND How now, what's the matter? Part!

KENT With you, goodman boy, if you please; come, I'll flesh ye;
come on, young master.   40

GLOUCESTER Weapons? Arms? What's the matter here?

CORNWALL Keep peace, upon your lives; he dies that strikes
again. What is the matter?

REGAN The messengers from our sister and the king?

CORNWALL What is your difference – speak!   45

OSWALD I am scarce in breath, my lord.

KENT No marvel, you have so bestirred your valour, you cowardly
rascal. Nature disclaims in thee: a tailor made thee.

CORNWALL Thou art a strange fellow – a tailor make a man?

KENT A tailor, sir, a stone-cutter, or a painter could not have made 50
him so ill, though they had been but two years o'th'trade.

CORNWALL Speak yet, how grew your quarrel?

OSWALD This ancient ruffian, sir, whose life I have spared at suit
of his grey beard –

*Kent is enraged by Oswald's lie, and attacks the sycophantic, dishonest
nature of great men's servants. Kent says that he dislikes Oswald's face, then
insults Cornwall, Regan and the others.*

1 Oswald the flatterer (in pairs)

Kent's tirade against Oswald is determined and direct. He threatens to
crush Oswald into mortar ('unbolted' means refined or effeminate), and
to daub him on the walls of a toilet ('jakes'). Kent attacks the dishonesty
of 'smiling rogues', saying that they are villains who undermine mar-
riages and family bonds ('holy cords'). Oswald is a flatterer who follows
the moods of his master, inflaming his passions ('being oil to fire') or
feeding his melancholy ('colder moods') with further depression. A flatterer is like a kingfisher ('halcyon') whose beak follows the direction of
the wind. Kent ends with an assault on Oswald's inane smiling ('epilep-
tic visage'), and threatens to drive him back to Camelot like a cackling
goose.

In line 78, Kent explains that no one could be more unlike Oswald
than he is ('No contraries hold more antipathy'). Using this idea of different personalities, talk together about why you think Kent detests
Oswald so vehemently.

2 Plain speaking

Kent says that he despises Oswald for his looks ('his countenance likes
me not' means I don't like his face). In lines 82–5, Kent extends this
criticism and plain-speaking to include everyone present. On stage, the
moment can be both electric and amusing, as the 'noble' characters take
in the meaning of Kent's blunt insult. Consider in turn, Kent,
Cornwall, Regan, Edmond and Gloucester. Suggest how each would
react as Kent speaks lines 82–5.

---

intrince tightly bound
smooth flatter
Renege deny
gall and vary irritation and mood-
    shift

visage face
Sarum Salisbury
Camelot legendary city of King
    Arthur, and possibly home of
    cackling geese

KENT Thou whoreson zed, thou unnecessary letter! My lord, if you   55
  will give me leave, I will tread this unbolted villain into mortar
  and daub the wall of a jakes with him. Spare my grey beard,
  you wagtail?
CORNWALL Peace, sirrah.
    You beastly knave, know you no reverence?   60
KENT Yes, sir, but anger hath a privilege.
CORNWALL Why art thou angry?
KENT That such a slave as this should wear a sword,
    Who wears no honesty. Such smiling rogues as these,
    Like rats, oft bite the holy cords a-twain,   65
    Which are too intrince t'unloose; smooth every passion
    That in the natures of their lords rebel,
    Being oil to fire, snow to the colder moods,
    Renege, affirm, and turn their halcyon beaks
    With every gall and vary of their masters,   70
    Knowing naught, like dogs, but following.
    A plague upon your epileptic visage!
    Smile you my speeches, as I were a fool?
    Goose, if I had you upon Sarum Plain,
    I'd drive ye cackling home to Camelot.   75
CORNWALL What, art thou mad, old fellow?
GLOUCESTER How fell you out? Say that.
KENT No contraries hold more antipathy
    Than I and such a knave.
CORNWALL   Why dost thou call him knave?
    What is his fault?
KENT   His countenance likes me not.   80
CORNWALL No more perchance does mine, nor his, nor hers.
KENT Sir, 'tis my occupation to be plain.
    I have seen better faces in my time
    Than stands on any shoulder that I see
    Before me at this instant.

Cornwall criticises Kent's blunt speaking. Kent uses exaggerated, courteous language, then claims truth in bluntness. Oswald lists Kent's actions against him. Cornwall decides to punish Kent in the stocks.

1 Blunt language, false language

Cornwall says that Kent pretends to be rough and rude well in excess of his true character ('quite from his nature'). Cornwall mocks such plain speaking, and suspects that Kent's bluntness is a mask, concealing more evil intentions than any number of flattering, anxious-to-please attendants ('silly ducking observants').

In lines 95–8, Kent deliberately mocks the insincere, deceitful language of false flatterers. He uses grandiloquent, pompous terms which are a parody of polite speech. In lines 99–102, Kent reverts to his customary plain, blunt manner of speaking. Speak both sets of Kent's lines to make the contrast between them as pronounced as you can.

2 Point it out! (in groups of three)

Take parts as Oswald, Kent and Lear. As Oswald reads aloud lines 104–13, everyone points at whoever is mentioned. For example, 'I (point to Oswald) never gave him (point to Kent) any', and so on.

3 Ajax – the final insult?

Kent's reference to Ajax may be the last straw in triggering Cornwall's anger. Ajax was a foolish Greek warrior renowned for his gullibility. The reference is also a pun on 'a jakes' meaning toilet.

---

constrains ... nature uses apparent bluntness for crafty purposes
stretch ... nicely bow and scrape too much in all they do
Phoebus' front the sun's forehead
dialect manner of speaking
very late most recently

misconstruction misunderstanding
compact in league with the king
deal of man macho attitude
For ... subdued for attacking a man who did not fight back
fleshment excitement

CORNWALL   This is some fellow   85
    Who, having been praised for bluntness, doth affect
    A saucy roughness, and constrains the garb
    Quite from his nature. He cannot flatter, he;
    An honest mind and plain, he must speak truth.
    And they will take it, so; if not, he's plain.   90
    These kind of knaves I know, which in this plainness
    Harbour more craft and more corrupter ends
    Than twenty silly-ducking observants
    That stretch their duties nicely.
KENT Sir, in good faith, in sincere verity,   95
    Under th'allowance of your great aspect,
    Whose influence like the wreath of radiant fire
    On flick'ring Phoebus' front –
CORNWALL   What mean'st by this?
KENT To go out of my dialect, which you discommend so much. I
    know, sir, I am no flatterer. He that beguiled you in a plain   100
    accent was a plain knave, which for my part I will not be,
    though I should win your displeasure to entreat me to't.
CORNWALL What was th'offence you gave him?
OSWALD I never gave him any.
    It pleased the king his master very late   105
    To strike at me upon his misconstruction,
    When he, compact, and flattering his displeasure,
    Tripped me behind; being down, insulted, railed,
    And put upon him such a deal of man
    That worthied him, got praises of the king   110
    For him attempting who was self-subdued,
    And in the fleshment of this dread exploit
    Drew on me here again.
KENT   None of these rogues and cowards
    But Ajax is their fool.
CORNWALL   Fetch forth the stocks!
    You stubborn, ancient knave, you reverend braggart,   115
    We'll teach you.

Kent protests against Cornwall's order to put him in the stocks, but Cornwall is unmoved, despite Gloucester's pleading. Gloucester commiserates with Kent, who accepts his punishment philosophically.

Kent in the stocks. In some productions, Oswald seizes the opportunity to get his own back on Kent. For example, in one production, Oswald removed Kent's boots; in another, he returned and urinated over Kent. Would Oswald attempt to get his own back on Kent in your production?

respects courtesy
selfsame colour same complexion
beseech beg

rubbed hindered, challenged
entreat plead

KENT   Sir, I am too old to learn:
Call not your stocks for me. I serve the king,
On whose employment I was sent to you.
You shall do small respects, show too bold malice
Against the grace and person of my master,   120
Stocking his messenger.
CORNWALL   Fetch forth the stocks!
As I have life and honour, there shall he sit till noon.
REGAN Till noon? Till night, my lord, and all night too.
KENT Why, madam, if I were your father's dog,
You should not use me so.
REGAN   Sir, being his knave, I will.   125
Stocks brought out
CORNWALL This is a fellow of the selfsame colour
Our sister speaks of. Come, bring away the stocks.
GLOUCESTER Let me beseech your grace not to do so.
The king his master needs must take it ill
That he, so slightly valued in his messenger,   130
Should have him thus restrained.
CORNWALL   I'll answer that.
REGAN My sister may receive it much more worse
To have her gentleman abused, assaulted.
[Kent is put in the stocks]
CORNWALL Come, my lord, away.
[Exeunt all but Gloucester and Kent]
GLOUCESTER I am sorry for thee, friend; 'tis the duke's pleasure, 135
Whose disposition all the world well knows
Will not be rubbed nor stopped. I'll entreat for thee.
KENT Pray do not, sir. I have watched and travelled hard.
Some time I shall sleep out, the rest I'll whistle.
A good man's fortune may grow out at heels.   140
Give you good morrow.
GLOUCESTER The duke's to blame in this; 'twill be ill taken. *Exit*

In the stocks, Kent reads a letter from Cordelia in which she promises to right all wrongs. Wearied, he sleeps. In Scene 3, Edgar plans to disguise himself as a mad beggar in an attempt to escape capture.

1 Cordelia's letter

Kent reads a letter he has received from Cordelia. She has been informed of Kent's disguise and of his activities ('obscurèd course'), and she intends to restore order to the country ('give losses their remedies'). Write Cordelia's letter.

2 Is Kent like Edgar?

In many productions, Kent remains on stage, sleeping silently as Edgar disguises himself to escape capture by his pursuers. Directors often choose to highlight the similarity between the two men here. After all, Shakespeare deliberately follows a soliloquy from the imprisoned Kent with one from the fugitive Edgar. Make a list of as many similarities between Kent and Edgar as you can identify.

3 Edgar as Tom o'Bedlam

In Shakespeare's time, mentally ill people were sent to the hospital of Bethlehem ('Bedlam') in London. When they were discharged, they lived by begging on the streets and wandering the countryside, often sticking sharp objects into their flesh in order to attract attention and charity. Such beggars were given the name 'Tom o'Bedlam'.

Edgar plans to reduce himself to an almost animal-like existence, wearing only a loin-cloth and tangling ('elf') all his hair. In some productions he removes his clothes and grimes himself with filth as he talks (see page 97). How would you stage lines 1–21 to show the way in which Edgar plans to adopt a new personality?

---

saw proverb
Thou ... sun you go from bad to good
thou beacon sun
Nothing ... misery only the most miserable witness miracles
enormous state wicked situation

o'er-watched exhausted
proclaimed publicly declared an outlaw
penury in contempt of man poverty, treating humanity with contempt
mortifièd dead to pain

KENT Good king, that must approve the common saw,
      Thou out of heaven's benediction com'st
      To the warm sun.   145
      Approach, thou beacon to this under globe,
      That by thy comfortable beams I may
      Peruse this letter. Nothing almost sees miracles
      But misery. I know 'tis from Cordelia,
      Who hath most fortunately been informed   150
      Of my obscurèd course, and shall find time
      For this enormous state, seeking to give
      Losses their remedies. All weary and o'er-watched,
      Take vantage, heavy eyes, not to behold
      This shameful lodging. Fortune, goodnight,   155
      Smile once more, turn thy wheel. [*He sleeps*]

ACT 2   SCENE 3
Open countryside near Gloucester's castle

Enter EDGAR

EDGAR I heard myself proclaimed,
      And by the happy hollow of a tree
      Escaped the hunt. No port is free, no place
      That guard and most unusual vigilance
      Does not attend my taking. Whiles I may 'scape   5
      I will preserve myself, and am bethought
      To take the basest and most poorest shape
      That ever penury in contempt of man
      Brought near to beast. My face I'll grime with filth,
      Blanket my loins, elf all my hairs in knots,   10
      And with presented nakedness outface
      The winds and persecutions of the sky.
      The country gives me proof and precedent
      Of Bedlam beggars, who with roaring voices
      Strike in their numbed and mortifièd arms,   15
      Pins, wooden pricks, nails, sprigs of rosemary;

75

Lear wonders why Cornwall and Regan were not at home to receive him. Seeing Kent in the stocks, the Fool mocks him, but Lear refuses to believe that Cornwall and Regan were responsible for such punishment.

1 'Edgar I nothing am'

Edgar's 'Poor Turlygod!' is his first attempt at speaking the nonsensical language of a mad beggar. In line 21, notice that Shakespeare again inserts the word 'nothing'. Just as Cordelia was told 'Nothing will come of nothing', Edgar, too, will come to nothing unless he adopts a new personality. However mean and lowly his disguise as Poor Tom, at least it gives Edgar the chance to survive. With what emphasis do you think that Edgar should speak 'nothing'?

2 Stage business?

The Fool jokes cuttingly about Kent's imprisonment, using a pun: 'nether-stocks' are stockings, but the expression also suggests the stocks which shackle Kent. Invent gestures and other stage business which the Fool could use to accompany lines 7–10.

3 Outdoing Lear (in pairs)

Take parts and speak lines 11–19. Each person tries to outdo the other, using gesture, as appropriate. Lear's words can be reinforced by movement, but Kent remains fixed in the stocks. Change parts and read again, first quickly, so that the exchange is rapid and quick-fire, then slowly and deliberately. Which version do you prefer? Why?

---

pelting paltry
lunatic bans mad curses
Enforce their charity beg for money
Mak'st ... pastime? is this your idea of a joke?

overlusty at legs keen to run away, oversexed
thy place mistook mistaken your status (as my messenger)
Jupiter chief of the Roman gods
Juno the moon goddess

And with this horrible object, from low farms,
Poor pelting villages, sheep-cotes, and mills,
Sometimes with lunatic bans, sometime with prayers,
Enforce their charity. 'Poor Turlygod! Poor Tom!'   20
That's something yet: Edgar I nothing am.   *Exit*

ACT 2   SCENE 4
The entrance to Gloucester's castle

Enter LEAR, FOOL, and GENTLEMAN

LEAR 'Tis strange that they should so depart from home
      And not send back my messenger.
GENTLEMAN   As I learned,
      The night before there was no purpose in them
      Of this remove.
KENT [*Waking*]   Hail to thee, noble master.
LEAR Ha!   5
      Mak'st thou this shame thy pastime?
KENT   No, my lord.
FOOL Ha, ha, he wears cruel garters. Horses are tied by the heads,
      dogs and bears by th'neck, monkeys by th'loins, and men by
      th'legs: when a man's overlusty at legs, then he wears wooden
      nether-stocks.   10
LEAR What's he that has so much thy place mistook
      To set thee here?
KENT   It is both he and she,
      Your son and daughter.
LEAR No.
KENT Yes.   15
LEAR No, I say.
KENT I say, yea.
LEAR By Jupiter, I swear no.
KENT By Juno, I swear ay.

Lear, angered by Kent's punishment, asks him to explain. Kent describes his cold reception and his recent clash with Oswald. The Fool speaks ominously of fortune favouring the wealthy.

1 Kent tells his story (in small groups)

Lear seems unwilling or unable to accept what Kent has told him. For Regan and Cornwall to put Kent in the stocks is 'worse than murder', as it is so blatantly disrespectful to Lear. Choose one of the following activities based on Kent's story in lines 24–42:

a One person reads the lines. The others, as Kent, Regan, Cornwall and Oswald, enact Kent's story.

b As one person reads the lines, another person, as the Fool, mimes all the events which Kent describes. Remember, the Fool may choose to exaggerate or mock whatever he hears.

c Lear makes no verbal response to Kent. Later, he complains of mounting hysteria, a choking feeling (lines 52–3). Make notes to show how Kent's words contribute, step by step, to this condition.

2 True or false?

The Fool continues his role as a chorus, commenting on, interpreting and evaluating what he sees. He expresses his thoughts in puzzling and teasing language, but with obvious reference to Lear's treatment by his daughters. He seems to suggest that fortune never favours ('ne'er turns the key to') the poor, and that poor fathers ('fathers that wear rags') will have unkind ('blind') children. With which of the three statements in lines 44–9 do you agree?

Resolve me explain to me
commend deliver
reeking post sweating messenger
spite of intermission in spite of interrupting me
meiny followers
Displayed behaved

more man than wit more courage than sense
Winter's ... way we're in for more bad weather (trouble ahead!)
bear bags are rich
dolours griefs, silver coins (dollars)
tell count

LEAR   They durst not do't:
          They could not, would not do't. 'Tis worse than murder,   20
          To do upon respect such violent outrage.
          Resolve me with all modest haste which way
          Thou mightst deserve or they impose this usage,
          Coming from us.
KENT   My lord, when at their home
          I did commend your highness' letters to them,   25
          Ere I was risen from the place that showed
          My duty kneeling, came there a reeking post,
          Stewed in his haste, half breathless, panting forth
          From Gonerill, his mistress, salutations;
          Delivered letters spite of intermission,   30
          Which presently they read. On those contents
          They summoned up their meiny, straight took horse,
          Commanded me to follow and attend
          The leisure of their answer, gave me cold looks;
          And meeting here the other messenger,   35
          Whose welcome I perceived had poisoned mine –
          Being the very fellow which of late
          Displayed so saucily against your highness –
          Having more man than wit about me, drew.
          He raised the house with loud and coward cries.   40
          Your son and daughter found this trespass worth
          The shame which here it suffers.
FOOL Winter's not gone yet, if the wild geese fly that way.
              Fathers that wear rags
                  Do make their children blind,   45
              But fathers that bear bags
                  Shall see their children kind.
              Fortune, that arrant whore,
              Ne'er turns the key to th'poor.
      But for all this, thou shalt have as many dolours for thy   50
      daughters as thou canst tell in a year.

Lear feels hysteria rising. He goes to find Regan. Kent asks why Lear has come with so few followers. The Fool speaks of the way in which men desert unsuccessful leaders, but claims he will remain faithful.

1 'Mother' – a 'climbing sorrow'

In Shakespeare's time, people believed that hysteria (the 'mother') originated in the pit of the stomach and rose through the body, affecting one part after another. (Lear calls it 'climbing sorrow' in line 53.) As you read on, think about the way in which Lear's rising anger and potential madness might be conveyed by all he speaks throughout Act 2.

2 Fair-weather friends

In lines 62–70, the Fool tells Kent of the folly of following a leader in decline. Kent could learn the folly of pointless labour from the proverbial ant, which will not try to seek food in the winter when there is none about. Even a blind man can smell the ill fortune ('him that's stinking') which accompanies a great man's fall from prosperity. Follow the 'great wheel' as it moves upwards, but get off as it spins downhill. That is the time when a hanger-on ('which serves and seeks for gain') will desert his master.

a The Fool's image is derived from the traditional wheel of fortune. Look out for further uses of the wheel of fortune image as you read through the play.

b If you were acting the part of the Fool, how would you want the audience to respond to your line 80?

---

mother hysteria
Hysterica passio! hysteria
element's place is
sir (line 71) man, servant
form show

perdy by God
fetches tricks
revolt and flying off rebellion and
  desertion

LEAR O how this mother swells up toward my heart!
    Hysterica passio! Down, thou climbing sorrow,
    Thy element's below. Where is this daughter?
KENT With the earl, sir, here within.
LEAR   Follow me not, stay here.   55
                                                  Exit
GENTLEMAN Made you no more offence but what you speak of?
KENT None.
    How chance the king comes with so small a number?
FOOL And thou hadst been set i'th'stocks for that question,
    thou'dst well deserved it.   60
KENT Why, fool?
FOOL We'll set thee to school to an ant, to teach thee there's no
    labouring i'th'winter. All that follow their noses are led by their
    eyes but blind men, and there's not a nose among twenty but
    can smell him that's stinking. Let go thy hold when a great   65
    wheel runs down a hill, lest it break thy neck with following.
    But the great one that goes upward, let him draw thee after.
    When a wise man gives thee better counsel, give me mine
    again; I would have none but knaves follow it, since a fool gives
    it.   70
            That sir which serves and seeks for gain
                And follows but for form,
            Will pack when it begins to rain
                And leave thee in the storm.
            But I will tarry, the fool will stay,   75
                And let the wise man fly;
            The knave turns fool that runs away,
                The fool no knave, perdy.
KENT Where learned you this, fool?
FOOL Not i'th'stocks, fool.   80

        Enter LEAR *and* GLOUCESTER

LEAR Deny to speak with me? They are sick, they are weary,
    They have travelled all the night? Mere fetches,
    The images of revolt and flying off.
    Fetch me a better answer.

Gloucester tries to excuse Cornwall's refusal to speak to Lear. At first, Lear is angry, then hesitant, but finally he demands that Regan and Cornwall appear. He fears the onset of madness.

1 Lear's angry words (in pairs)

To experience Lear's changing moods, try one or more of the following activities on what he says in lines 88–114:

a Read aloud Lear's lines as you walk around the room. Change direction at every punctuation mark.

b One person reads all Lear's lines aloud. After each punctuation mark, the other says 'calmer' or 'angrier' to indicate Lear's changing emotions.

c Decide what movements or gestures Lear could use to accompany his words.

d Rate Lear's moods on a scale of 1–10 (1 for calm, 10 for violently angry). Draw a graph to show the ups and downs of his temper.

2 Cockney fools

The Fool gives two examples of acts of foolish kindness. The cockney (a Londoner) cook could not bear to kill eels before cooking them in a pie, so she 'put 'em i'th'paste alive'. She had to hit them on the head ('knapped 'em o'th'coxcombs') when they tried to escape. Her brother put butter on his horse's hay as a treat, without realising that horses dislike grease and fat. Think about why the Fool tells these two stories. Is he trying to cheer up Lear, or to remind him of his folly, or to paint a picture of a world going mad? Or … ?

Infirmity … bound illness makes us neglect our duties
forbear cease my command
fallen … will no longer in sympathy with my headstrong impulse
sickly fit ill person

remotion aloofness, refusal
practice trickery
presently instantly
paste pastry
knapped hit
coxcombs heads

GLOUCESTER   My dear lord,
         You know the fiery quality of the duke,   85
         How unremovable and fixed he is
         In his own course.
LEAR Vengeance, plague, death, confusion!
         'Fiery'? What 'quality'? Why Gloucester, Gloucester,
         I'd speak with the Duke of Cornwall and his wife.   90
GLOUCESTER Well, my good lord, I have informed them so.
LEAR 'Informed them'? Dost thou understand me, man?
GLOUCESTER Ay, my good lord.
LEAR The king would speak with Cornwall, the dear father
         Would with his daughter speak! Commands – tends –
             service!   95
         Are they 'informed' of this? My breath and blood!
         'Fiery'? The 'fiery duke'? Tell the hot duke that –
         No, but not yet; maybe he is not well:
         Infirmity doth still neglect all office
         Whereto our health is bound. We are not ourselves   100
         When nature, being oppressed, commands the mind
         To suffer with the body. I'll forbear,
         And am fallen out with my more headier will,
         To take the indisposed and sickly fit
         For the sound man. – Death on my state! Wherefore   105
         Should he sit here? This act persuades me
         That this remotion of the duke and her
         Is practice only. Give me my servant forth.
         Go tell the duke and's wife I'd speak with them,
         Now, presently: bid them come forth and hear me,   110
         Or at their chamber door I'll beat the drum
         Till it cry sleep to death.
GLOUCESTER I would have all well betwixt you.   *Exit*
LEAR Oh me, my heart! My rising heart! But down.
FOOL Cry to it, nuncle, as the cockney did to the eels when she put   115
     'em i'th'paste alive; she knapped 'em o'th'coxcombs with a stick
     and cried, 'Down, wantons, down!' 'Twas her brother that in
     pure kindness to his horse buttered his hay.

*Kent is freed from the stocks. Lear criticises Gonerill's treatment of him.
Regan defends her sister, and says that Lear needs guidance in his old age.
Lear mocks the suggestion to apologise to Gonerill.*

---

1 A frosty greeting? (in groups of four)

Even very short, simple sentences and clipped, precise language can contain a wealth of possibilities for actors to interpret and perform. Using lines 119–20 only, stage the entrance of Cornwall and Regan, and the greetings they exchange with Lear. How does Lear say his five words, Cornwall his four and Regan her seven?

2 'Like a vulture here'

Lines 126–7 refer to the legend of Prometheus, who was tortured by a vulture gnawing at his liver. Use the image to design a poster advertising a production of *King Lear*.

3 Naming Regan

In lines 121–9, Lear uses Regan's name four times. You will find that he continues to use it many times later in the scene. Do you agree with those critics who say that he has recovered a sense of affection for her, or do you think that there are other explanations?

4 'Unsightly tricks'

Regan reminds her father that his natural course of life is near its limit (lines 138–40). She says that he should ask Gonerill's forgiveness. Lear responds sarcastically in lines 144–8. Try different ways of performing Lear's lines to discover how his kneeling and language make Regan see his behaviour as the awkward and embarrassing 'unsightly tricks' of an elderly relative.

Sepulch'ring entombing, containing buried within
naught wicked
You less … duty she appreciates her duty more than you appreciate her worth

confine limit
house family
vouchsafe give
raiment clothes

Enter CORNWALL, REGAN, GLOUCESTER, [*and*] *Servants*

LEAR Good morrow to you both.
CORNWALL   Hail to your grace.
                     Kent here set at liberty
REGAN I am glad to see your highness.   120
LEAR Regan, I think you are. I know what reason
        I have to think so. If thou shouldst not be glad,
        I would divorce me from thy mother's tomb,
        Sepulch'ring an adultress. [*To Kent*] O are you free?
        Some other time for that. Belovèd Regan,   125
        Thy sister's naught. Oh Regan, she hath tied
        Sharp-toothed unkindness, like a vulture here –
        I can scarce speak to thee – thou'lt not believe
        With how depraved a quality – oh Regan!
REGAN I pray you, sir, take patience. I have hope   130
        You less know how to value her desert
        Than she to scant her duty.
LEAR   Say? How is that?
REGAN I cannot think my sister in the least
        Would fail her obligation. If, sir, perchance
        She have restrained the riots of your followers,   135
        'Tis on such ground and to such wholesome end
        As clears her from all blame.
LEAR   My curses on her.
REGAN O sir, you are old,
        Nature in you stands on the very verge
        Of his confine. You should be ruled and led   140
        By some discretion that discerns your state
        Better than you yourself. Therefore I pray you
        That to our sister you do make return;
        Say you have wronged her.
LEAR   Ask her forgiveness?
        Do you but mark how this becomes the house?   145
        [*Kneels*] 'Dear daughter, I confess that I am old;
        Age is unnecessary: on my knees I beg
        That you'll vouchsafe me raiment, bed, and food.'
REGAN Good sir, no more: these are unsightly tricks.
        Return you to my sister.

Lear refuses to stay with Gonerill, cursing her ingratitude and ill treatment of him. Lear says that Regan is a better, more natural daughter than Gonerill. A trumpet heralds Gonerill's arrival.

1 Lear curses Gonerill

Lear rehearses his grievances against Gonerill. She has reduced his followers by half, scowled at him ('Looked black upon me'), and lashed him verbally, striking at his heart and his love.

Identify all the curses which Lear directs at Gonerill in lines 154–60, and speak them as powerfully and dramatically as you can.

2 The arithmetic of love (in pairs)

Lear's language shows how selfishly he quantifies and calculates his love. In Act 1, he demanded of his daughters, 'Which of you shall we say doth love us most?', pitting the daughters against each other in a competitive test of their love. Now his hatred of Gonerill is born of his belief that she has not appropriately acknowledged her debt of love to her father, halving his followers. Even his language to Regan, whom he says he will never curse, expresses the arithmetic of love ('grudge', 'cut', 'scant', 'offices', 'bond', 'effects', 'dues', 'half').

Read lines 166–74 to each other, highlighting any words or phrases which express Lear's calculating view of love.

3 Regan's reply

Regan responds briefly to Lear's flattering words: 'Good sir, to th'purpose'. Suggest how you think Regan's reply should be spoken on stage.

---

abated deprived	**scant my sizes** cut my allowances
train followers	**oppose the bolt** lock the door
top head	**offices** duties
young bones unborn child	**Effects** necessary requirements
You taking airs you evil vapours	**approves** confirms

LEAR [*Rising*]   Never, Regan.   150
    She hath abated me of half my train,
    Looked black upon me, struck me with her tongue
    Most serpent-like upon the very heart.
    All the stored vengeances of heaven fall
    On her ingrateful top! Strike her young bones,   155
    You taking airs, with lameness.
CORNWALL   Fie, sir, fie.
LEAR You nimble lightnings, dart your blinding flames
    Into her scornful eyes! Infect her beauty,
    You fen-sucked fogs, drawn by the powerful sun
    To fall and blister.   160
REGAN O the blessed gods! So will you wish on me
    When the rash mood is on.
LEAR No, Regan, thou shalt never have my curse.
    Thy tender-hefted nature shall not give
    Thee o'er to harshness. Her eyes are fierce, but thine   165
    Do comfort and not burn. 'Tis not in thee
    To grudge my pleasures, to cut off my train,
    To bandy hasty words, to scant my sizes,
    And in conclusion, to oppose the bolt
    Against my coming in. Thou better know'st   170
    The offices of nature, bond of childhood,
    Effects of courtesy, dues of gratitude.
    Thy half o'th'kingdom hast thou not forgot
    Wherein I thee endowed.
REGAN   Good sir, to th'purpose.
LEAR Who put my man i'th'stocks?
                   Tucket within
CORNWALL   What trumpet's that?   175
REGAN I know't, my sister's. This approves her letter
    That she would soon be here.

            Enter OSWALD

              Is your lady come?

Lear is shaken by Regan's warm greeting of Gonerill. Regan advises Lear to return to Gonerill, reducing his followers by half. Lear lists the hardships and ignominies which he would rather endure.

1 Lear's isolation

Stage directors often seize the opportunity to use Gonerill's entrance as a means of emphasising Lear's growing isolation. Characters are 'blocked' (grouped) to show their allegiances.

When Gonerill arrives, Regan takes her by the hand in a show of friendship. Gonerill chooses her words carefully to give offence to Lear, referring to his 'indiscretion' and 'dotage'. Cornwall also lines up against Lear, confirming that Kent was punished on his orders. Kent, the Gentleman, the Fool and Gloucester, all possible allies of Lear, are on stage but do not speak.

Imagine that you are directing the play. Work out how to 'block' Gonerill's entrance in order to underline Lear's vulnerability in the face of his daughters' hostility.

2 What would Lear rather do? (in pairs)

In lines 200–10, Lear specifies three ordeals which he would prefer to endure rather than return to Gonerill. Choose one and make a tableau to represent it. Invite other pairs to identify which ordeal you have chosen.

3 'Necessity's sharp pinch'

Lear imagines a life like the wolf and the owl, suffering hostility from exposure to the raw elements. His image in line 204 is of physical pain ('pinch') inflicted upon him by another of his grim, cruel companions, 'Necessity' (the most bare existence). As you read on, you will discover that Lear's imagined ordeal becomes all too real.

---

easy-borrowed quickly put on
sway influence
indiscretion lack of judgement
dotage foolish old age
sides chest
abjure reject

enmity o'th'air fierce storms
knee kneel before
squire-like like a servant
afoot intact
sumpter pack-horse

LEAR This is a slave whose easy-borrowed pride
    Dwells in the sickly grace of her he follows.
    Out, varlet, from my sight!
CORNWALL   What means your grace?   180

           Enter GONERILL

LEAR Who stocked my servant? Regan, I have good hope
    Thou didst not know on't. Who comes here? O heavens!
    If you do love old men, if your sweet sway
    Allow obedience, if you yourselves are old,
    Make it your cause; send down and take my part.   185
    [*To Gonerill*] Art not ashamed to look upon this beard?
    O Regan, will you take her by the hand?
GONERILL Why not by th'hand, sir? How have I offended?
    All's not offence that indiscretion finds,
    And dotage terms so.
LEAR   O sides, you are too tough!   190
    Will you yet hold? How came my man i'th'stocks?
CORNWALL I set him there, sir; but his own disorders
    Deserved much less advancement.
LEAR   You? Did you?
REGAN I pray you, father, being weak, seem so.
    If till the expiration of your month   195
    You will return and sojourn with my sister,
    Dismissing half your train, come then to me.
    I am now from home and out of that provision
    Which shall be needful for your entertainment.
LEAR Return to her? and fifty men dismissed?   200
    No, rather I abjure all roofs and choose
    To wage against the enmity o'th'air,
    To be a comrade with the wolf and owl,
    Necessity's sharp pinch. Return with her?
    Why, the hot-blooded France, that dowerless took   205
    Our youngest born – I could as well be brought
    To knee his throne and, squire-like, pension beg
    To keep base life afoot. Return with her?
    Persuade me rather to be slave and sumpter
    To this detested groom.
GONERILL   At your choice, sir.   210

Lear curses Gonerill and renounces her. He decides to stay with Regan with his hundred followers. Regan gives her reasons for rejecting Lear's proposal, and says that she will accept only twenty-five knights.

1 'My daughter ... a disease' (in pairs)

Although Gonerill is his daughter ('thou art my flesh, my blood, my daughter'), Lear curses her in lines 214–18 using the language of bodily corruption: 'disease', 'boil', 'plague-sore', 'embossèd carbuncle' (swollen tumour). Once again, Shakespeare contrasts the natural and healthy order of family life with the corrupt, distorting infection of Gonerill's 'unnatural' behaviour. Talk together about the way in which Gonerill might react on hearing herself described as a disease.

2 Like father, like daughter (in groups of three)

Just as Lear's love is measured and calculating, so his sense of self-esteem seems to be in direct proportion to the number of his knights. Now he is experiencing the consequences of his arithmetical way of judging value. Regan and Gonerill cruelly pay their father back in kind, measuring their love for him by numbers.

Take parts and speak lines 223–56 emphasising all words connected with numbers.

3 'I gave you all'

Lear's very simple, clear language in line 243 carries huge emotional weight. Try different ways of speaking the line in order to capture a variety of Lear's possible moods. For example, he could be furious, despairing, astonished, disbelieving, full of pathos or ...

thunder-bearer Jupiter (Jove), the Greek god who was armed with thunderbolts
shoot fire thunderbolts
mingle ... passion think rationally about your impulsive behaviour

avouch it declare it true
sith since
charge expense
slack ye serve you negligently
depositaries trustees

LEAR I prithee, daughter, do not make me mad.
     I will not trouble thee, my child. Farewell.
     We'll no more meet, no more see one another.
     But yet thou art my flesh, my blood, my daughter,
     Or rather a disease that's in my flesh,   215
     Which I must needs call mine. Thou art a boil,
     A plague-sore, or embossèd carbuncle
     In my corrupted blood. But I'll not chide thee;
     Let shame come when it will, I do not call it.
     I do not bid the thunder-bearer shoot,   220
     Nor tell tales of thee to high-judging Jove.
     Mend when thou canst, be better at thy leisure;
     I can be patient, I can stay with Regan,
     I and my hundred knights.
REGAN   Not altogether so.
     I looked not for you yet, nor am provided   225
     For your fit welcome. Give ear, sir, to my sister,
     For those that mingle reason with your passion
     Must be content to think you old, and so –
     But she knows what she does.
LEAR   Is this well spoken?
REGAN I dare avouch it, sir. What, fifty followers?   230
     Is it not well? What should you need of more?
     Yea, or so many, sith that both charge and danger
     Speak 'gainst so great a number? How in one house
     Should many people under two commands
     Hold amity? 'Tis hard, almost impossible.   235
GONERILL Why might not you, my lord, receive attendance
     From those that she calls servants, or from mine?
REGAN Why not, my lord? If then they chanced to slack ye,
     We could control them. If you will come to me
     (For now I spy a danger) I entreat you   240
     To bring but five and twenty; to no more
     Will I give place or notice.
LEAR I gave you all.
REGAN   And in good time you gave it.
LEAR Made you my guardians, my depositaries,
     But kept a reservation to be followed   245
     With such a number. What, must I come to you
     With five and twenty? Regan, said you so?

Lear engages in the arithmetic of love, but his daughters' reductive calculations devastate him. He deliberates on humanity's basic needs, and swears revenge against his daughters. He fears for his sanity.

1 'O reason not the need!' (in groups of five or six)

Lear's final outburst has several elements:

lines 257–63 Human need cannot be determined by precise calculation. If our requirements are no more than the very basic necessities, then a human life is worth no more than an animal's. Regan's fine clothes are superfluous to her natural needs.

lines 264–71 Pleading for patience, Lear calls upon the gods to inspire him to noble and manly anger against his daughters.

lines 271–5 Lear issues a terrifying but confused threat against his daughters.

lines 275–9 Lear claims that nothing will make him weep. He fears that he will go mad.

a Decide to whom Lear is addressing the lines (for example, both sisters, only one sister, the gods, the Fool).

b Make a guess at how Lear was going to define 'true need' before he stopped himself at line 263.

c Lear identifies his prime need as patience. Share your ideas about what you think is his most pressing need at this moment.

d Take turns at speaking lines 271–5 in different ways. Is Lear's threat terrifying, pathetic, or …?

---

tend attend, serve
Our basest … superfluous our poorest people, even with the little they have, have more than they need

flaws splinters, fragments
Or ere before

REGAN And speak't again, my lord. No more with me.
LEAR Those wicked creatures yet do look well-favoured
   When others are more wicked. Not being the worst   250
   Stands in some rank of praise. [*To Gonerill*] I'll go with
    thee;
   Thy fifty yet doth double five and twenty,
   And thou art twice her love.
GONERILL   Hear me, my lord:
   What need you five and twenty? ten? or five?
   To follow in a house where twice so many   255
   Have a command to tend you?
REGAN   What need one?
LEAR O reason not the need! Our basest beggars
   Are in the poorest thing superfluous.
   Allow not nature more than nature needs,
   Man's life is cheap as beast's. Thou art a lady;   260
   If only to go warm were gorgeous,
   Why nature needs not what thou gorgeous wear'st,
   Which scarcely keeps thee warm. But for true need –
   You heavens, give me that patience, patience I need.
   You see me here, you gods, a poor old man,   265
   As full of grief as age, wretched in both;
   If it be you that stirs these daughters' hearts
   Against their father, fool me not so much
   To bear it tamely. Touch me with noble anger,
   And let not women's weapons, water drops,   270
   Stain my man's cheeks. No, you unnatural hags,
   I will have such revenges on you both
   That all the world shall – I will do such things –
   What they are, yet I know not, but they shall be
   The terrors of the earth! You think I'll weep;   275
   No, I'll not weep,
       Storm and tempest
   I have full cause of weeping, but this heart
   Shall break into a hundred thousand flaws
   Or ere I'll weep. O fool, I shall go mad.
    Exeunt [Lear, Gloucester, Kent, Gentleman, and Fool]

Regan and Gonerill agree that they will welcome Lear but not his followers. Gloucester fears for Lear's well-being, but Regan and Cornwall insist that Gloucester closes his doors against Lear and the storm.

Regan and Cornwall. In many productions, Regan and Cornwall are portrayed as physically attractive. Think about why such productions choose to emphasise their good looks, and suggest how you would want to present them.

1 Learning the hard way?

Regan believes that headstrong men must learn their lesson from the harms they bring on themselves (lines 295–7). What is your view?

bestowed accommodated
put himself from rest deprived
 himself of comfort
For his particular as for him
but will ... whither but I've no idea
 where he intends to go

ruffle blow, rage
a desperate train his riotous
 knights
incense incite, provoke
being apt ... abused Lear being
 susceptible to lies and flattery

CORNWALL Let us withdraw; 'twill be a storm.   280
REGAN This house is little. The old man and's people
    Cannot be well bestowed.
GONERILL 'Tis his own blame; hath put himself from rest
    And must needs taste his folly.
REGAN For his particular, I'll receive him gladly,   285
    But not one follower.
GONERILL   So am I purposed.
    Where is my lord of Gloucester?
CORNWALL Followed the old man forth.

Enter GLOUCESTER

              He is returned.
GLOUCESTER The king is in high rage.
CORNWALL   Whither is he going?
GLOUCESTER He calls to horse, but will I know not whither.   290
CORNWALL 'Tis best to give him way; he leads himself.
GONERILL My lord, entreat him by no means to stay.
GLOUCESTER Alack, the night comes on, and the high winds
    Do sorely ruffle; for many miles about
    There's scarce a bush.
REGAN   O sir, to wilful men,   295
    The injuries that they themselves procure
    Must be their schoolmasters. Shut up your doors.
    He is attended with a desperate train,
    And what they may incense him to, being apt
    To have his ear abused, wisdom bids fear.   300
CORNWALL Shut up your doors, my lord; 'tis a wild night,
    My Regan counsels well: come out o'th'storm.

                      Exeunt

Looking back at Act 2

Activities for groups or individuals

1 Storm clouds gather

In Shakespeare's plays, a storm often mirrors the disorder within individual minds or society. Identify instances of either individual or social disturbance in each of the four scenes in Act 2. Display your findings in an appropriate way, for example by drawings or a collage of quotations.

2 Old age

Gonerill and Regan find their father's erratic behaviour perplexing and demanding. They are greatly provoked by Lear's capricious and unpredictable ways. Working in groups of four, talk together about whether or not you think that old people can be difficult to handle, especially for young people. Then take roles as Lear, Gonerill, Regan and a family guidance counsellor. It is the counsellor's task to interview father and daughters about the disagreements and tensions between them.

3 Goodness

The forces of wickedness gather momentum in Act 2, although a few signs of hope flicker, suggesting that 'goodness' is still at work in Lear's Britain. Find at least one example of goodness, the hope of a better future, in each of the four scenes.

4 The Fool's jingles

Choose any of the Fool's songs or jingles from Act 2. Decide which aspect you want to emphasise, rehearse it, and present it in an appropriate way.

5 Points of view

Talk together about the extent to which you agree with the students who wrote the following statements:

- 'Lear's curses against his daughters are both terrifying and pathetic.'
- 'Regan's line 256 in Scene 4 ('What need one?') is the cruellest line in *King Lear*.'

Edgar adopts his disguise as Poor Tom. Remind yourself of lines 9–12 in Scene
3, and compare this picture with that on page 120.

The Gentleman describes Lear raging at the storm. Kent recounts the French spies' reports of growing rivalry between Albany and Cornwall. Kent gives the Gentleman a ring to take to Cordelia.

1 Who is the Gentleman?

Several anonymous characters (the Gentleman, the Knight and the Captain) make fleeting appearances in the play. The Gentleman's dramatic function seems to be two-fold: to ensure that the audience hears important information, and to prepare for the appearance of Lear and the Fool in the next scene. His comment that he is 'minded like the weather' is Shakespeare's reminder that the troubled affairs of the kingdom are reflected in people's minds and in the raging storm.

Make up an identity for the Gentleman. Describe his reaction to meeting a man who entrusts him with secret information and gives him a special ring to take to Lear's banished daughter.

2 A film story-board (in pairs)

This short scene tells of Lear in the storm, of Albany and Cornwall's political rivalry, of the French intelligence operation against the British, and of the harsh treatment ('hard rein') given to Lear. In the quarto version (see page 232), additional lines provide a striking description of Lear in the storm and news of the French invasion.

If the scene were filmed, imagine what the audience would see if lines 3–21 were used as a voice-over to accompanying images. Make a story-board of your ideas, showing each camera shot and using appropriate words, phrases or lines as captions.

Contending with struggling against
fretful elements stormy weather
main mainland
labours to out-jest tries to make a joke of
upon ... Commend on the evidence of my eyes I trust

speculations Intelligent secret agents
snuffs huffs, grudges
packings conspiracies
furnishings surface details
out-wall appearance

ACT 3   SCENE 1
Near Gloucester's castle

Storm still. Enter KENT *(disguised) and a* GENTLEMAN, *severally*

KENT Who's there, besides foul weather?
GENTLEMAN One minded like the weather, most unquietly.
KENT I know you. Where's the king?
GENTLEMAN Contending with the fretful elements;
    Bids the wind blow the earth into the sea,   5
    Or swell the curlèd waters 'bove the main,
    That things might change or cease.
KENT   But who is with him?
GENTLEMAN None but the fool, who labours to out-jest
    His heart-struck injuries.
KENT   Sir, I do know you,
    And dare upon the warrant of my note   10
    Commend a dear thing to you. There is division,
    Although as yet the face of it is covered
    With mutual cunning, 'twixt Albany and Cornwall,
    Who have – as who have not, that their great stars
    Throned and set high? – servants, who seem no less,   15
    Which are to France the spies and speculations
    Intelligent of our state. What hath been seen,
    Either in snuffs and packings of the dukes,
    Or the hard rein which both of them hath borne
    Against the old kind king; or something deeper,   20
    Whereof, perchance, these are but furnishings –
GENTLEMAN I will talk further with you.
KENT   No, do not.
    For confirmation that I am much more
    Than my out-wall, open this purse and take
    What it contains. If you shall see Cordelia –   25
    As fear not but you shall – show her this ring,
    And she will tell you who that fellow is
    That yet you do not know. Fie on this storm!
    I will go seek the king.

Kent and the Gentleman separate to find Lear. Lear rages furiously with the
storm, demanding that it destroy humankind. He ignores the Fool's request
for shelter, and accuses the storm of joining forces with his daughters.

1 The storm (in small groups)

Explore the drama of the storm through one or more of the following activities:

a Create the storm. Share out lines 1–9 and memorise them. Experiment with voices and movement to present your own interpretation of the chaos and confusion of the storm.

b Storm images. Consider each of the first nine lines in turn and describe the pictures which they conjure up in your mind.

c Is the storm in Lear's head? The storm created by Lear's broken family gives way to the real storm on the heath outside Gloucester's castle. The violent weather reflects not only events in the story, but also the state of Lear's mind. Identify the lines which suggest that Lear has descended into madness.

d Do you feel sorry for Lear? Lines 19 and 22–3 show Lear seemingly self-pitying. Does he succeed in gaining your sympathy?

e Staging the storm. The audience must feel that they are watching and hearing a violent tempest, but they must also be able to hear every word that is spoken. Work out how you would stage lines 1–23 for greatest dramatic effect.

f 'Crack nature's moulds'. In lines 7–9, Lear calls for the destruction of the world. Design a theatre programme cover based on this image.

---

to effect in importance
cataracts and hurricanoes
  waterfalls and waterspouts
cocks weather-cocks
thought-executing mind-numbing,
  swifter than thought

Vaunt-couriers forerunners
thick rotundity round-belliedness
germens seeds
court holy water flattery
subscription loyalty
high-engendered sky born

GENTLEMAN Give me your hand. Have you no more to say?   30
KENT Few words, but to effect more than all yet:
        That when we have found the king – in which your pain
        That way, I'll this – he that first lights on him
        Holla the other.

Exeunt

ACT 3   SCENE 2
The heath near Gloucester's castle

Storm still. Enter LEAR and FOOL

LEAR Blow, winds, and crack your cheeks! Rage, blow,
        You cataracts and hurricanoes, spout
        Till you have drenched our steeples, drowned the cocks!
        You sulph'rous and thought-executing fires,
        Vaunt-couriers of oak-cleaving thunderbolts,   5
        Singe my white head; and thou all-shaking thunder,
        Strike flat the thick rotundity o'th'world,
        Crack nature's moulds, all germens spill at once
        That makes ingrateful man.
FOOL O nuncle, court holy water in a dry house is better than this   10
    rain-water out o'door. Good nuncle, in, ask thy daughters
    blessing. Here's a night pities neither wise men nor fools.
LEAR Rumble thy bellyful; spit, fire; spout, rain!
        Nor rain, wind, thunder, fire are my daughters.
        I tax not you, you elements, with unkindness.
        I never gave you kingdom, called you children.   15
        You owe me no subscription. Then let fall
        Your horrible pleasure. Here I stand your slave,
        A poor, infirm, weak, and despised old man;
        But yet I call you servile ministers,   20
        That will with two pernicious daughters join
        Your high-engendered battles 'gainst a head
        So old and white as this. O, ho! 'tis foul.

The Fool sings of the foolishness of sexual excess. Kent fears for Lear's safety in this worst-ever storm. Lear calls on the gods to use the storm to reveal all hidden crimes.

1 The Fool's jibes

The Fool's song is full of sexual innuendo. 'Codpiece', 'head', 'head-piece' and 'toe' were all slang words for penis. The Fool is satirising uncontrolled sex and the diseases which result, as well as criticising Lear's irresponsible behaviour which has led to his homelessness. Lear responds to the Fool's teasing by promising patience and saying 'nothing' (that word again!).

Identify the jibes in lines 24–34 which you think would pierce Lear's conscience most sharply.

2 The power of the storm (in small groups)

In Shakespeare's time, the play would have been performed in daylight, so he provides the actors with words which enable them to create the atmosphere of a dark, tempestuous night. Share a group reading of lines 40–7, stressing the words which convey the power of the storm at night.

3 More sinned against?

Lear lists those wrong-doers who should fear the storm's ferocity, because it will reveal to the gods their enemies: unpunished criminals, liars, sex hypocrites and murderers. Do you think that Lear's self-assessment in lines 57–8 is accurate? Compile two lists to show Lear's sins and the sins against him, and make your own judgement about whether you think he is 'more sinned against than sinning'.

---

house have sex
louse catch a sexually transmitted
  disease
grace majesty
Gallow terrify
affliction effect
pudder turmoil

Caitiff wretch
seeming hypocrisy
Rive ... continents burst out of
  your bodies
cry ... grace beg for mercy (a
  summoner was a court official)

FOOL He that has a house to put 's head in has a good head-piece.
    [*Sings*] The codpiece that will house   25
            Before the head has any,
      The head and he shall louse;
            So beggars marry many.
      The man that makes his toe
            What he his heart should make,   30
      Shall of a corn cry woe,
            And turn his sleep to wake.
  For there was never yet fair woman but she made mouths in
  a glass.

           Enter KENT [*disguised*]

LEAR No, I will be the pattern of all patience.   35
    I will say nothing.
KENT Who's there?
FOOL Marry, here's grace and a codpiece; that's a wise man and a
  fool.
KENT Alas, sir, are you here? Things that love night   40
    Love not such nights as these. The wrathful skies
    Gallow the very wanderers of the dark
    And make them keep their caves. Since I was man
    Such sheets of fire, such bursts of horrid thunder,
    Such groans of roaring wind and rain I never   45
    Remember to have heard. Man's nature cannot carry
    Th'affliction nor the fear.
LEAR   Let the great gods,
    That keep this dreadful pudder o'er our heads,
    Find out their enemies now. Tremble, thou wretch,
    That hast within thee undivulgèd crimes   50
    Unwhipped of justice. Hide thee, thou bloody hand,
    Thou perjured and thou simular of virtue
    That art incestuous. Caitiff, to pieces shake,
    That under covert and convenient seeming
    Has practised on man's life. Close pent-up guilts,   55
    Rive your concealing continents and cry
    These dreadful summoners grace. I am a man
    More sinned against than sinning.

Kent urges Lear to rest in a nearby hovel. Kent proposes to return to the castle to ask for shelter for the king. The Fool's prophecy promises mixed fortunes for Britain.

1 The magic of poverty (in small groups)

In lines 67–9, Lear remarks on the way in which the most ordinary, basic needs of shelter and warmth are made precious by poverty. But will he learn from having to manage with the meanest of comforts when he is in the hovel? Try to recall an occasion on which you yourself were grateful for food, warmth or shelter.

2 The Fool's song and prophecy

a In one film version, as the Fool sang lines 72–5, the camera cut to Lear's daughters feasting in front of a blazing fire. They sat in silence, listening to the Fool's plaintive voice outside in the storm. Suggest what reasons the director may have had for showing this scene while the Fool is singing.

b The Fool makes a bizarre prediction that corruption, immorality and unhappiness will come to Britain ('Albion'), followed by a golden age in which customary evils will be reversed (lines 85–92). Write your own prediction of what will happen to Lear. Try to use rhyming couplets in the same style as the Fool, listing first the bad events, and then the good. You could begin like this:

When a king casts out his honest child
When he walks the heath in weather wild
When men misjudge their kith and kin
When it seems that evil will surely win

---

scanted mean, neglected
courtesan prostitute
matter deed
cutpurses pickpockets
throngs crowded places
usurers ... field money-lenders do
    business in public

bawds pimps
That going ... feet everything will
    be normal
Merlin wizard to the legendary
    King Arthur

KENT   Alack, bare-headed?
    Gracious my lord, hard by here is a hovel.
    Some friendship will it lend you 'gainst the tempest.   60
    Repose you there, while I to this hard house –
    More harder than the stones whereof 'tis raised,
    Which even but now, demanding after you,
    Denied me to come in – return and force
    Their scanted courtesy.
LEAR   My wits begin to turn.   65
    Come on, my boy. How dost, my boy? Art cold?
    I am cold myself. – Where is this straw, my fellow?
    The art of our necessities is strange,
    And can make vile things precious. Come, your hovel. –
    Poor fool and knave, I have one part in my heart   70
    That's sorry yet for thee.
FOOL [*Sings*] He that has and a little tiny wit,
                With heigh-ho, the wind and the rain,
            Must make content with his fortunes fit,
                Though the rain it raineth every day.   75
LEAR True, boy. – Come, bring us to this hovel.
                                [Exeunt Lear and Kent]
FOOL This is a brave night to cool a courtesan. I'll speak a pro-
    phecy ere I go:
            When priests are more in word than matter;
            When brewers mar their malt with water;   80
            When nobles are their tailors' tutors,
            No heretics burned, but wenches' suitors,
            Then shall the realm of Albion
            Come to great confusion.
            When every case in law is right;   85
            No squire in debt nor no poor knight;
            When slanders do not live in tongues,
            Nor cutpurses come not to throngs;
            When usurers tell their gold i'th'field,
            And bawds and whores do churches build,   90
            Then comes the time, who lives to see't,
            That going shall be used with feet.
    This prophecy Merlin shall make, for I live before his time.
                                                    Exit

Gloucester has been forbidden to help Lear. He tells of a secret letter about an armed invasion to support the king, and proposes to go to Lear. But the treacherous Edmond plans to betray his father.

1 Where do they meet?

Gloucester tells Edmond of the growing opposition to Cornwall and his allies. To be overheard would be fatal. The suggested location for this scene is a private room in Gloucester's castle, but no one really knows where Shakespeare intended the scene to be set. Decide where and how you would set the scene to suggest Gloucester's fear of being overheard.

2 Edmond's irony

Some members of the audience might smile knowingly at Edmond's outrage in line 6. Do you think that the actor playing Edmond should emphasise the word 'unnatural' to bring out an ironic echo of Gloucester's line 1?

3 Language matches emotion (in small groups)

Gloucester's lines 7–17 are a disjointed succession of short sentences and broken phrases. Read the lines around the group, changing over at each punctuation mark. Repeat the reading, trying to bring out the urgency of the situation by adding gesture and different tones of voice. Talk together about what Gloucester's style of speaking suggests about his state of mind.

leave permission	**privily** secretly
perpetual everlasting	**perceived** noticed
entreat plead	**toward** to come
sustain help	**deserving** reward
footed landed	**draw** win
incline to side with	

ACT 3 SCENE 3
A room in Gloucester's castle

Enter GLOUCESTER *and* EDMOND

GLOUCESTER Alack, alack, Edmond, I like not this unnatural
dealing. When I desired their leave that I might pity him, they
took from me the use of mine own house, charged me on pain
of perpetual displeasure neither to speak of him, entreat for
him, or any way sustain him.   5

EDMOND Most savage and unnatural!

GLOUCESTER Go to, say you nothing. There is division between
the dukes, and a worse matter than that. I have received a letter
this night – 'tis dangerous to be spoken – I have locked the
letter in my closet. These injuries the king now bears will be   10
revenged home. There is part of a power already footed. We
must incline to the king. I will look him and privily relieve him.
Go you and maintain talk with the duke, that my charity be not
of him perceived. If he ask for me, I am ill and gone to bed. If I
die for it – as no less is threatened me – the king my old master   15
must be relieved. There is strange things toward, Edmond;
pray you be careful.   *Exit*

EDMOND This courtesy, forbid thee, shall the duke
    Instantly know, and of that letter too.
    This seems a fair deserving, and must draw me   20
    That which my father loses: no less than all.
    The younger rises when the old doth fall.   *Exit*

Kent urges Lear to enter the hovel. Lear refuses, saying that he cannot feel the storm because the mental pain caused by his daughters is more severe. He insists that the Fool goes in before him.

1 Filial ingratitude – Lear's 'greater malady' (in large groups)

In lines 6–21, Lear explains why the storm does not torment him as much as the hurt caused by his daughters ('filial ingratitude'). He is so obsessed by the pain of his daughters' hostility and disrespect that he is numb to the effects of the tempest. Only someone free of mental worries has the time to think about bodily discomforts ('When the mind's free / The body's delicate').

To explore Lear's feelings, one student plays Kent. All the others play Lear and stand in a circle around Kent. Kent asks each Lear to enter speaking line 22 ('Good my lord, enter here'). Each Lear refuses, using any one of the remarks from lines 6–22. The Lears should vary their tone and add gestures, deciding whether they speak to Kent, to the daughters, or to the storm. Which responses does Kent have most difficulty in understanding?

2 'In, boy, go first' (in pairs)

Compare line 26 with lines 66–71 in Act 3 Scene 2. Discuss what the comparison suggests about Lear's growth of concern for others.

Wilt will you
contentious angry
malady illness, torment
scarce hardly
shun avoid
filial daughterly

frank honest
Prithee please
ease rest
leave ... more the chance to think about more painful things

Act 3 Scene 4
Outside a hovel on the heath

Enter LEAR, KENT *(disguised), and* FOOL

KENT Here is the place, my lord. Good my lord, enter.
    The tyranny of the open night's too rough
    For nature to endure.
                    Storm still
LEAR   Let me alone.
KENT Good my lord, enter here.
LEAR   Wilt break my heart?
KENT I had rather break mine own. Good my lord, enter.   5
LEAR Thou think'st 'tis much that this contentious storm
    Invades us to the skin: so 'tis to thee.
    But where the greater malady is fixed,
    The lesser is scarce felt. Thou'dst shun a bear,
    But if thy flight lay toward the roaring sea,   10
    Thou'dst meet the bear i'th'mouth. When the mind's free,
    The body's delicate. This tempest in my mind
    Doth from my senses take all feeling else,
    Save what beats there: filial ingratitude.
    Is it not as this mouth should tear this hand   15
    For lifting food to't? But I will punish home.
    No, I will weep no more. In such a night
    To shut me out? Pour on, I will endure.
    In such a night as this! O Regan, Gonerill,
    Your old kind father, whose frank heart gave all –   20
    O that way madness lies; let me shun that;
    No more of that.
KENT   Good my lord, enter here.
LEAR Prithee, go in thyself, seek thine own ease.
    This tempest will not give me leave to ponder
    On things would hurt me more; but I'll go in.   25
    In, boy, go first. You houseless poverty –
    Nay, get thee in; I'll pray, and then I'll sleep.
                             Exit [Fool]

Lear prays for the homeless and starving, whom he has neglected until now. The Fool rushes from the hovel, fearful and crying for help. Edgar, as Poor Tom, speaks madly of being tormented by the devil.

1 Lear's prayer

Many people believe that lines 28–36 mark a turning-point in Lear's spiritual development. After years of absolute rule, he now begins to pity the poor and homeless and to realise his neglect ('O I have ta'en too little care of this').

a Experiment with appropriate ways of staging lines 28–36. It could be an elaborate ceremony with Kent joining in, a private prayer heard only by the audience, or a way of your choosing.

b Collect contemporary newspaper photographs of the poor and homeless for a montage wall display under the title of 'poor naked wretches'. Use some of Lear's other words as captions.

2 Poor Tom's raving (in small groups)

As Poor Tom, Edgar uses the language of madness, veering from sense to nonsense. Don't feel you have to understand everything he says. (After all, who knows what 'do, de, do, de, do, de' means?) His dislocated language adds to the chaotic atmosphere of the scene, and his appearance can shock the audience.

In lines 49–54, Edgar describes how he was tempted to suicide by 'the foul fiend'. Use improvisation to explore Tom's raving. One person reads the lines, the others react to him as passers-by in a street might react to a homeless down-and-out.

bide endure	**pew** porch, balcony
looped and windowed tattered	**ratsbane** rat poison
physic medicine	**ride … bridges** ride over narrow
pomp royalty	bridges
shake the superflux discard	**five wits** intelligence, senses
unnecessary possessions	**star-blasting** diseases caused by the
halters hangman's nooses	stars

Poor naked wretches, wheresoe'er you are
That bide the pelting of this pitiless storm,
How shall your houseless heads and unfed sides,   30
Your looped and windowed raggedness defend you
From seasons such as these? O I have ta'en
Too little care of this. Take physic, pomp,
Expose thyself to feel what wretches feel,
That thou mayst shake the superflux to them   35
And show the heavens more just.

Enter FOOL

EDGAR [*Within*] Fathom and half; fathom and half; poor Tom!
FOOL Come not in here, nuncle! Here's a spirit! Help me, help
me!
KENT Give me thy hand. Who's there?   40
FOOL A spirit, a spirit! He says his name's Poor Tom.
KENT What art thou that dost grumble there i'th'straw? Come
forth.

[*Enter* EDGAR, *disguised as a madman*]

EDGAR Away, the foul fiend follows me. Through the sharp
hawthorn blow the winds. Humh! Go to thy bed and warm   45
thee.
LEAR Didst thou give all to thy daughters? And art thou come to
this?
EDGAR Who gives anything to Poor Tom, whom the foul fiend
hath led through fire and through flame, through ford and   50
whirlpool, o'er bog and quagmire; that hath laid knives under
his pillow and halters in his pew; set ratsbane by his porridge;
made him proud of heart to ride on a bay trotting-horse over
four-inched bridges, to course his own shadow for a traitor.
Bless thy five wits, Tom's a-cold! O do, de, do, de, do de. Bless   55
thee from whirlwinds, star-blasting, and taking. Do Poor Tom
some charity, whom the foul fiend vexes. There could I have
him now, and there, and there again, and there.
Storm still

Lear assumes that Tom's madness has been caused by unkind daughters. Tom offers a mangled version of the Ten Commandments, and then parodies the seven deadly sins in his story of his past life as a lustful servingman.

1 Lear's obsession with daughters continues
(in groups of three)

Lear blames Tom's condition on his experience as a father of 'pelican daughters'. It was believed the pelican fed on the flesh of its parents. Lear seems unable to identify any other cause for Tom's madness than daughters. Take parts and read aloud lines 59–70. Echo or repeat every mention of fathers or daughters. To what extent would you want the actor playing Lear to emphasise such 'daughter' words in performance?

2 The story of Poor Tom (in groups of four or five)

There is a danger of reading too much into the disjointed thoughts in lines 77–90. For example, some critics suggest that Tom is imitating the sound of the wind at 'suum' and 'mun', and pretending to ride an imaginary horse at 'Dauphin ... *cessez*!'. But who really knows? However, his story can illuminate the themes and situations in the play. Tom appears to parody the Ten Commandments and the seven deadly sins.

a One person reads aloud lines 77–90, pausing frequently for the others to illustrate the tale with a series of tableaux.

b Much of Tom's story is concerned with illicit sexual behaviour, such as having an affair with his mistress and using prostitutes. Why do you think Edgar has Tom show so much sexual disgust? Talk together about Edgar's possible motives for this aspect of Tom's character.

---

pass predicament
Nay ... shamed no, he kept a
  blanket to save our blushes
the plagues ... air the diseases in
  the atmosphere
light land

commit ... array don't commit
  adultery or desire fine clothing
outparamoured outwhored, had
  more lovers than
sloth idleness
plackets slits in petticoats

LEAR What, has his daughters brought him to this pass?

Couldst thou save nothing? Wouldst thou give 'em all? 60

FOOL Nay, he reserved a blanket, else we had been all shamed.

LEAR Now all the plagues that in the pendulous air

Hang fated o'er men's faults, light on thy daughters!

KENT He hath no daughters, sir.

LEAR Death, traitor! Nothing could have subdued nature 65

To such a lowness but his unkind daughters.

Is it the fashion that discarded fathers

Should have thus little mercy on their flesh?

Judicious punishment: 'twas this flesh begot

Those pelican daughters. 70

EDGAR Pillicock sat on Pillicock Hill; alow, alow, loo, loo.

FOOL This cold night will turn us all to fools and madmen.

EDGAR Take heed o'th'foul fiend, obey thy parents, keep thy
words' justice, swear not, commit not with man's sworn spouse,
set not thy sweet heart on proud array. Tom's a-cold. 75

LEAR What hast thou been?

EDGAR A servingman, proud in heart and mind, that curled my
hair, wore gloves in my cap, served the lust of my mistress'
heart, and did the act of darkness with her. Swore as many
oaths as I spake words, and broke them in the sweet face of 80
heaven. One that slept in the contriving of lust and waked to
do it. Wine loved I dearly, dice dearly, and in woman outparamoured the Turk. False of heart, light of ear, bloody of
hand; hog in sloth, fox in stealth, wolf in greediness, dog in
madness, lion in prey. Let not the creaking of shoes nor the 85
rustling of silks betray thy poor heart to woman. Keep thy foot
out of brothels, thy hand out of plackets, thy pen from lender's
books, and defy the foul fiend. Still through the hawthorn
blows the cold wind, says suum, mun, nonny. Dauphin, my boy,
boy, *cessez!* let him trot by. 90

Storm still

*Lear regards Poor Tom as the embodiment of the natural state of humanity.
He attempts to remove his own clothes in imitation. Edgar, as Tom, speaks of
demons and nightmares, and tells Gloucester of his suffering.*

1 'The thing itself'

Lear continues to be preoccupied with Tom: the greatest in the kingdom admires the least. He sees Tom, 'the thing itself', as showing
humanity's fundamental nature: a 'poor, bare, forked animal', naked or
'unaccommodated' by the material trappings of life. Speak lines 91–7,
then suggest why the traumatised king wishes to remove his clothes,
and how the other characters react to Lear's attempts to undress.

2 Poor Tom's language (in small groups)

Shakespeare probably borrowed much of Poor Tom's language from a
book on witchcraft, Samuel Harsnett's *A Declaration of Egregious Popish
Impostures*, published in 1603 (see page 205). For example, Edgar calls
Gloucester 'Flibbertigibbet', a dancing devil which stalks the earth at
night, spreading disease and deformity amongst all living things. He
then chants about St Swithin meeting the nightmare, a female monster
who suffocated her victims with her great weight. St Swithin orders her
to 'alight' (get off), makes her 'troth plight' (promise not to do it again),
and tells her to clear off ('aroint thee').

a Prepare a group performance of lines 102–10, exploring different
   ways of speaking or singing Tom's words.

b In lines 115–25, Edgar details Tom's life as a down-and-out on the
   heath. He refers to a past life of comfort when he possessed many
   clothes. One person speaks the lines, the others provide suitable
   actions to accompany each detail.

---

ow'st owe
on's of us (line 95), of his (line 100)
forked two-legged
lendings clothes
naughty wicked
old lecher's dirty old man's
web and the pin cataracts in the eye

mildews the white rots the ripe
creature creatures
Swithold ... wold St Swithin walks
  over open country three times
mantle slime
tithing parish
Smulkin devil

LEAR Thou wert better in a grave than to answer with thy uncovered body this extremity of the skies. Is man no more than this? Consider him well. Thou ow'st the worm no silk, the beast no hide, the sheep no wool, the cat no perfume. Ha! Here's three on's are sophisticated; thou art the thing itself. Unaccommodated man is no more but such a poor, bare, forked animal as thou art. Off, off, you lendings! Come, unbutton here. 95

FOOL Prithee, nuncle, be contented; 'tis a naughty night to swim in. Now a little fire in a wild field were like an old lecher's heart – a small spark, all the rest on's body cold. Look, here comes a walking fire. 100

Enter GLOUCESTER *with a torch*

EDGAR This is the foul Flibbertigibbet; he begins at curfew and walks till the first cock. He gives the web and the pin, squints the eye, and makes the harelip; mildews the white wheat, and hurts the poor creature of earth. 105
[*Chants*]   Swithold footed thrice the wold,
          He met the nightmare and her ninefold;
                Bid her alight
                And her troth plight,
          And aroint thee, witch, aroint thee! 110

KENT How fares your grace?

LEAR What's he?

KENT Who's there? What is't you seek?

GLOUCESTER What are you there? Your names?

EDGAR Poor Tom, that eats the swimming frog, the toad, the tadpole, the wall-newt, and the water; that in the fury of his heart, when the foul fiend rages, eats cowdung for salads, swallows the old rat and the ditch-dog, drinks the green mantle of the standing pool; who is whipped from tithing to tithing, and stocked, punished, and imprisoned; who hath had three suits to his back, six shirts to his body, 115 120
                Horse to ride, and weapon to wear;
                But mice and rats and such small deer
                Have been Tom's food for seven long year.
Beware my follower. Peace, Smulkin; peace, thou fiend! 125

Gloucester tries to persuade Lear to leave for a place of safety, but Lear is more interested in learning wisdom from Poor Tom. Gloucester tells of his love for Edgar. The king shows compassion for Poor Tom.

1 Tom the philosopher

In lines 127–8, Tom speaks of more of Harsnett's devils (see page 205). Modo is the Devil, and Mahu the organiser of Hell. Tom twice complains of the cold, perhaps to avoid or attract his father's attention. Despite the poor naked man's bizarre language and behaviour, Lear's preoccupation with Tom continues. On three occasions Lear calls Tom a philosopher. Suggest reasons why he attributes such great wisdom to a down-and-out.

2 Dramatic irony (in pairs)

Just as Lear could not recognise the true nature of his own daughters until they turned on him, so Gloucester displays similar blindness. He laments the loss of Kent and Edgar, but fails to recognise them when they are right in front of him.

The poignancy of this scene is deepened by the dramatic irony of the two disguised characters listening to their real identities being discussed. Twice Gloucester draws a parallel between his own family problems and those of the king (lines 129–30 and 150–4). He also expresses love for Edgar. In lines 147–8, Gloucester mentions 'good Kent', and affirms that his stand against the king has been vindicated.

Share a reading of lines 147–55, and as either Kent or Edgar, speak your thoughts at the moments you are mentioned. Talk together about how Gloucester's lack of perception affects your view of his character.

---

flesh ... it our children have become wicked and hate us, their parents
injunction order
Theban Greek scholar (the ancient Greeks were famous for their learning)

Importune implore
His wits ... unsettle he's cracking up
outlawed from my blood declared an outlaw and disinherited
beseech beg

GLOUCESTER What, hath your grace no better company?
EDGAR The Prince of Darkness is a gentleman. Modo he's called,
    and Mahu.
GLOUCESTER Our flesh and blood, my lord, is grown so vile,
        That it doth hate what gets it.   130
EDGAR Poor Tom's a-cold.
GLOUCESTER Go in with me. My duty cannot suffer
        T'obey in all your daughters' hard commands.
        Though their injunction be to bar my doors
        And let this tyrannous night take hold upon you,   135
        Yet have I ventured to come seek you out
        And bring you where both fire and food is ready.
LEAR First let me talk with this philosopher.
        What is the cause of thunder?
KENT Good my lord, take his offer; go into th'house.   140
LEAR I'll talk a word with this same learnèd Theban.
        What is your study?
EDGAR How to prevent the fiend, and to kill vermin.
LEAR Let me ask you one word in private.
KENT Importune him once more to go, my lord.   145
        His wits begin t'unsettle.
GLOUCESTER   Canst thou blame him?
                Storm still
        His daughters seek his death. Ah, that good Kent,
        He said it would be thus, poor banished man!
        Thou sayst the king grows mad; I'll tell thee, friend,
        I am almost mad myself. I had a son,   150
        Now outlawed from my blood; he sought my life
        But lately, very late. I loved him, friend;
        No father his son dearer. True to tell thee,
        The grief hath crazed my wits. What a night's this!
        I do beseech your grace –
LEAR   O, cry you mercy, sir. –   155
        Noble philosopher, your company.
EDGAR Tom's a-cold.
GLOUCESTER In, fellow, there, in t'hovel; keep thee warm.
LEAR Come, let's in all.
KENT   This way, my lord.
LEAR   With him;
        I will keep still with my philosopher.   160

The king's party enters the hovel. Edmond shows Cornwall the letter implicating Gloucester in the French invasion plans. Cornwall promises Edmond his father's title and orders him to help in Gloucester's arrest.

1 Out of the storm

Stage directors often end a scene with exits which express the mood that has been developed in that scene. Decide how you would stage the exit of Lear and his followers. For each character, suggest the movements and expressions which you think convey their feelings most dramatically.

2 Tom the story-teller (in pairs)

Edgar's final lines refer to two medieval stories. Child Roland is the knightly hero of a twelfth-century tale, *Chanson de Roland*, and may also have featured in a version of *Jack the Giant-killer*. The 'dark tower' in Tom's story could be Gloucester's castle. Lines 167–8 are still well-known and much used. Talk together about what Tom's parting words suggest might happen in the play. Also decide how and to whom Edgar speaks: to his father, to the audience, to himself in his own voice, or … ?

3 Edmond the manipulator (in pairs)

Feigning self-reproach for his disloyalty, Edmond betrays his father to Cornwall. Take parts and try reading lines 1–21 in various tones to bring out Edmond's deceitful nature. Don't forget that his aside to the audience is the only moment in which he expresses his true thoughts and feelings.

---

censured judged
nature family love
something fears somewhat frightens
a provoking … himself an understandable fault caused by Gloucester's evil

approves him … party proves him a spy
apprehension arrest
stuff his increase Cornwall's
persever continue, persevere
blood family ties

KENT Good my lord, soothe him; let him take the fellow.
GLOUCESTER Take him you on.
KENT Sirrah, come on. Go along with us.
LEAR Come, good Athenian.
GLOUCESTER No words, no words. Hush.   165
EDGAR Child Roland to the dark tower came.
      His word was still 'Fie, fo, and fum;
      I smell the blood of a British man.'

Exeunt

ACT 3   SCENE 5
A room in Gloucester's castle

Enter CORNWALL and EDMOND

CORNWALL I will have my revenge ere I depart his house.
EDMOND How, my lord, I may be censured, that nature thus gives
    way to loyalty, something fears me to think of.
CORNWALL I now perceive it was not altogether your brother's evil
    disposition made him seek his death, but a provoking merit set   5
    a-work by a reprovable badness in himself.
EDMOND How malicious is my fortune, that I must repent to be
    just! This is the letter which he spoke of, which approves him
    an intelligent party to the advantages of France. O heavens, that
    this treason were not, or not I the detector!   10
CORNWALL Go with me to the duchess.
EDMOND If the matter of this paper be certain, you have mighty
    business in hand.
CORNWALL True or false, it hath made thee Earl of Gloucester.
    Seek out where thy father is, that he may be ready for our   15
    apprehension.
EDMOND [Aside] If I find him comforting the king, it will stuff his
    suspicion more fully. – I will persever in my course of loyalty,
    though the conflict be sore between that and my blood.
CORNWALL I will lay trust upon thee, and thou shalt find a dearer   20
    father in my love.

Exeunt

Gloucester leaves to find provisions for Lear and his followers. Edgar continues his talk of devils, but briefly drops his disguise. The Fool poses a puzzling question. In his mental anguish, Lear imagines revenge.

Madness on the heath. From left to right: the Fool, Kent, Edgar as Poor Tom, Lear. In the quarto version of the play, Lear stages a mock trial of Gonerill and Regan after line 14. Turn to page 233 and read the additional lines. If you were putting on the play, would you include the trial scene in your production? Give reasons for your decision.

piece out the comfort make it
   more comfortable
Frateretto a dancing devil
Nero … darkness Nero, the
   villainous Roman emperor, is
   damned in hell

yeoman small landowner or farmer
   (this might be a private joke about
   Shakespeare's own family)
spits spikes for roasting meat
mar … counterfeiting spoil my
   acting

ACT 3   SCENE 6
Inside the hovel on the heath

Enter KENT *(disguised) and* GLOUCESTER

GLOUCESTER Here is better than the open air; take it thankfully. I
   will piece out the comfort with what addition I can. I will not be
   long from you.
KENT All the power of his wits have given way to his impatience;
   the gods reward your kindness!   5

Exit [Gloucester]

Enter LEAR, EDGAR *[disguised as a madman], and* FOOL

EDGAR Frateretto calls me, and tells me Nero is an angler in the
   lake of darkness. Pray, innocent, and beware the foul fiend.
FOOL Prithee, nuncle, tell me whether a madman be a gentleman
   or a yeoman.
LEAR A king, a king!   10
FOOL No, he's a yeoman that has a gentleman to his son; for he's a
   mad yeoman that sees his son a gentleman before him.
LEAR To have a thousand with red burning spits
   Come hizzing in upon 'em!
EDGAR Bless thy five wits.   15
KENT O pity! Sir, where is the patience now
   That you so oft have boasted to retain?
EDGAR *[Aside]* My tears begin to take his part so much
   They mar my counterfeiting.
LEAR The little dogs and all,   20
   Tray, Blanch, and Sweetheart – see, they bark at me.

Tom speaks a verse of warning to all dogs. Lear broods on Regan's ingratitude, then falls asleep. Gloucester tells of a plot to assassinate the king. He urges Kent to take Lear to safety at Dover.

1 Tom's rhyme

Lines 22–30 are Tom's response to Lear's vision of his pet dogs. Try speaking his rhyme as a charm or incantation.

2 Theatrical links (in pairs)

In the theatre, a director can use striking stage business to link together apparently unconnected aspects of the play. 'Anatomise' (line 33) means to dissect a corpse. In one production, the director used Lear's 'Let them anatomise Regan' to show why the Fool disappears from the play altogether after this scene. Lear acted out his line with a sword, and mortally wounded the Fool by stabbing him through a cushion which the Fool was holding across his stomach. Share your opinions about this action linking Regan and the Fool, and decide how you would have the Fool speak his last line.

3 Gloucester to the rescue (in groups of three)

Gloucester is anxious for Lear to escape quickly, since he has overheard a plan to kill Lear. Share a reading of lines 44–53, changing readers at each punctuation mark. Try to emphasise the urgency in Gloucester's words.

4 A soliloquy for Edgar?

The quarto version of the play includes a soliloquy for Edgar to end Scene 6. Turn to page 234 and decide whether or not you would include it in your own production. Give reasons for your decision.

Avaunt be gone	**horn** begging cup
brach bitch	**Persian** fancy, exotic
Bobtail tyke dog with no tail	**litter** coach with closed curtains
trundle-tail dog with curly tail	**Stand ... loss** are bound to die
hatch door	**that ... conduct** who will quickly
wakes festivals	lead you to safety

EDGAR Tom will throw his head at them. – Avaunt, you curs!
        Be thy mouth or black or white,
        Tooth that poisons if it bite,
        Mastiff, greyhound, mongrel grim,   25
        Hound or spaniel, brach or him,
        Bobtail tyke or trundle-tail,
        Tom will make him weep and wail;
        For with throwing thus my head,
        Dogs leap the hatch, and all are fled.   30
Do, de, de, de. *Cessez!* Come, march to wakes and fairs and
market towns. Poor Tom, thy horn is dry.
LEAR Then let them anatomise Regan; see what breeds about her
heart. Is there any cause in nature that makes these hard-
hearts? [*To Edgar*] You, sir, I entertain for one of my hundred,   35
only I do not like the fashion of your garments. You will say
they are Persian; but let them be changed.
KENT Now, good my lord, lie here and rest a while.
LEAR Make no noise, make no noise. Draw the curtains: so, so.
    We'll go to supper i'th'morning. [*He sleeps*]   40
FOOL And I'll go to bed at noon.

           Enter GLOUCESTER

GLOUCESTER Come hither, friend. Where is the king my master?
KENT Here, sir, but trouble him not; his wits are gone.
GLOUCESTER Good friend, I prithee take him in thy arms.
    I have o'erheard a plot of death upon him.   45
    There is a litter ready. Lay him in't
    And drive toward Dover, friend, where thou shalt meet
    Both welcome and protection. Take up thy master;
    If thou shouldst dally half an hour, his life
    With thine and all that offer to defend him   50
    Stand in assurèd loss. Take up, take up,
    And follow me, that will to some provision
    Give thee quick conduct. Come, come away.
                              Exeunt

Cornwall says that the French army has invaded. He instructs Edmond to leave to avoid witnessing his father's harsh punishment. Oswald reports that some of Gloucester's followers have gone to Dover with Lear.

1 'Pluck out his eyes' (in pairs)

The two sisters do not hesitate to suggest ghastly penalties for Edmond's father. In Shakespeare's time, the usual punishment for a duke's crime was beheading. As you read on, you will find out how quickly and terrifyingly Gonerill's order becomes action.

2 Edmond reflects on his good fortune

Edmond says nothing in this scene. He has manoeuvred himself into a powerful position (and close to Gonerill). He now hears Cornwall call him 'my lord of Gloucester'. Remind yourself of Edmond's first soliloquy (Act 1 Scene 2), in which he declared his will to succeed. Then write an aside (of four to six lines) for him to be spoken after line 12.

3 Oswald – another man on the make (in pairs)

Kent called Oswald 'superserviceable' (Act 2 Scene 2, line 16), because he will serve anybody if it is to his advantage. In the seemingly neutral lines 14–19, Oswald is only giving information, but an actor would still attempt to convey Oswald's ambition. Try several readings of the lines to find a version which will bring out Oswald's sycophantic nature.

Post ride
sister sister-in-law
beholding sight
festinate preparation hasty gearing-up for war

bound to the like going to do the same
posts messengers
Hot questrists fast riders

ACT 3 SCENE 7
The Great Hall of Gloucester's castle

Enter CORNWALL, REGAN, GONERILL, EDMOND *and Servants*

CORNWALL [*To Gonerill*] Post speedily to my lord your husband;
show him this letter. The army of France is landed. – Seek out
the traitor Gloucester.

                                  [*Exeunt some Servants*]

REGAN Hang him instantly.

GONERILL Pluck out his eyes.   5

CORNWALL Leave him to my displeasure. Edmond, keep you our
sister company. The revenges we are bound to take upon your
traitorous father are not fit for your beholding. Advise the
duke, where you are going, to a most festinate preparation:
we are bound to the like. Our posts shall be swift and intel-   10
ligent betwixt us. Farewell, dear sister; farewell, my lord of
Gloucester.

               [*Gonerill and Edmond start to leave*]

                    Enter OSWALD

How now, where's the king?

OSWALD My lord of Gloucester hath conveyed him hence.
    Some five or six and thirty of his knights,   15
    Hot questrists after him, met him at gate,
    Who, with some other of the lord's dependants,
    Are gone with him toward Dover, where they boast
    To have well-armèd friends.

CORNWALL Get horses for your mistress.   20

                                   [*Exit Oswald*]

Cornwall will vent his anger on Gloucester without restraint of the law.
Gloucester is brought in and tied to a chair. He protests that his captors are
breaking the customs of hospitality, but his interrogation begins.

1 Power without responsibility

In lines 24–7, Cornwall admits that he should not execute Gloucester
without a proper trial, but he has the power to do so without others pre-
venting him. His anger overrides all other considerations ('shall do a
curtsy to our wrath'). Make a list of examples from history or current
affairs when the abuse of power has produced similar atrocities.

2 Customs of hospitality

Regan and Cornwall are cruel to their host Gloucester in word and
action. But in Shakespeare's time, the roles of host and guest were
invested with special significance. To infringe the code of conduct
between host and guest was almost sinful. In *Macbeth*, Shakespeare portrays the terrible consequences of breaking the laws of hospitality, when
Macbeth murders his guest, King Duncan, who is, like Gloucester, an
old man.

Cornwall orders Gloucester to be bound to a chair, and Regan offers
the insult of pulling hairs out of the old man's beard. Gloucester twice
protests about his guests' abuse of his hospitality, but Cornwall and
Regan's malice and threats continue unabated as they accuse Gloucester
of treachery. As you read to the end of the scene, keep in mind the
notion of a host assaulted by his guests as yet another example of the
unnatural behaviour which the play explores.

Pinion bind
pass ... justice sentence him to
  death without trial
do a curtsy ... wrath bow down to
  our anger
corky dry and withered

ravish pluck
quicken come to life
ruffle molest
confederacy conspiracy
Late footed recently landed

GONERILL Farewell, sweet lord, and sister.
CORNWALL Edmond, farewell.

>   [*Exeunt Gonerill and Edmond*]
>   [*To Servants*]   Go seek the traitor Gloucester.
>   Pinion him like a thief; bring him before us.
>   [*Exeunt other Servants*]
>   Though well we may not pass upon his life
>   Without the form of justice, yet our power   25
>   Shall do a curtsy to our wrath, which men
>   May blame but not control.

>   *Enter* GLOUCESTER *and Servants*

>   Who's there – the traitor?

REGAN Ingrateful fox! 'tis he.
CORNWALL Bind fast his corky arms.
GLOUCESTER What means your graces? Good my friends, con-
>   sider   30
>   You are my guests. Do me no foul play, friends.
CORNWALL Bind him, I say.
REGAN   Hard, hard! O filthy traitor!
GLOUCESTER Unmerciful lady as you are, I'm none.
CORNWALL To this chair bind him. Villain, thou shalt find –

>   [*Regan plucks Gloucester's beard*]

GLOUCESTER By the kind gods, 'tis most ignobly done,   35
>   To pluck me by the beard.
REGAN So white, and such a traitor?
GLOUCESTER   Naughty lady,
>   These hairs which thou dost ravish from my chin
>   Will quicken and accuse thee. I am your host.
>   With robbers' hands my hospitable favours   40
>   You should not ruffle thus. What will you do?
CORNWALL Come, sir, what letters had you late from France?
REGAN Be simple-answered, for we know the truth.
CORNWALL And what confederacy have you with the traitors
>   Late footed in the kingdom?
REGAN   To whose hands   45
>   You have sent the lunatic king. Speak.

Gloucester admits that he sent Lear to safety in Dover. He hopes to see Lear's enemies receive just punishment. Cornwall gouges out one of the old man's eyes. A servant challenges Cornwall.

1 Gloucester tied to the stake

The image in line 53 is of the cruel Elizabethan 'sport' of bear-baiting. A bear was chained to a stake, and dogs were set upon it in a series of attacks known as 'the course'. Bets were taken on the outcome of the fight. Bear-baiting was hugely popular. There was a bear-baiting pit next to Shakespeare's Globe Theatre and a street there is still called Bear Gardens. Think of a modern image which also captures the vulnerability of the old man and the cruelty of his interrogators.

2 Gloucester defies his tormentors (in small groups)

In lines 55–65, Gloucester bravely justifies his actions. His words are rich in imagery of holiness, biting, sea-storms, tears, wolf howls and 'wingèd vengeance'. Strangely, Cornwall and Regan do not interrupt him. Talk about why you think Shakespeare chose to give Gloucester eleven uninterrupted lines. Consider their dramatic purpose: how they recall central themes in the play, help establish the mood of the scene, and prepare for Gloucester's own tragedy.

3 Creating dramatic tension (in groups of three)

Many members of the audience suffer almost unbearable discomfort in this scene. But their discomfort does not simply arise from the action of the blinding. Shakespeare uses language to heighten dramatic tension before Cornwall attacks Gloucester's eyes. Re-read lines 46–71 and suggest some of the ways in which words are used to create dramatic tension.

---

guessingly set down written without knowing the facts
anointed holy, kingly
boarish pig-like
buoyed risen
stellèd starry

holp helped (by weeping)
All cruels else subscribe let dangerous animals in, but not Lear
wingèd vengeance the revenge of the gods

GLOUCESTER I have a letter guessingly set down,
    Which came from one that's of a neutral heart,
    And not from one opposed.
CORNWALL   Cunning.
REGAN   And false.
CORNWALL Where hast thou sent the king?
GLOUCESTER   To Dover.   50
REGAN Wherefore to Dover? Wast thou not charged at peril –
CORNWALL Wherefore to Dover? Let him answer that.
GLOUCESTER I am tied to th'stake, and I must stand the course.
REGAN Wherefore to Dover?
GLOUCESTER Because I would not see thy cruel nails   55
    Pluck out his poor old eyes, nor thy fierce sister
    In his anointed flesh stick boarish fangs.
    The sea, with such a storm as his bare head
    In hell-black night endured, would have buoyed up
    And quenched the stellèd fires.   60
    Yet, poor old heart, he holp the heavens to rain.
    If wolves had at thy gate howled that stern time,
    Thou shouldst have said, 'Good porter, turn the key:
    All cruels else subscribe.' But I shall see
    The wingèd vengeance overtake such children.   65
CORNWALL See't shalt thou never. Fellows, hold the chair.
    Upon these eyes of thine I'll set my foot.
GLOUCESTER He that will think to live till he be old,
    Give me some help! – O cruel! O you gods!
        [Cornwall puts out one of Gloucester's eyes]
REGAN One side will mock another: th'other, too.   70
CORNWALL If you see vengeance –
SERVANT   Hold your hand, my lord.
    I have served you ever since I was a child,
    But better service have I never done you
    Than now to bid you hold.
REGAN   How now, you dog!

Regan kills the servant. Cornwall blinds Gloucester's other eye. Regan tauntingly informs Gloucester of Edmond's treachery. She orders Gloucester to be thrown out. Cornwall says he is badly wounded.

1 'Tender-hefted' Regan? (in groups of four)

Lear described Regan as 'tender-hefted' (Act 2 Scene 4, line 164), yet she takes part in a barbaric maiming and kills a servant. She then taunts Gloucester, saying that Edmond has betrayed him (lines 86–9). Take parts and work together to decide how Regan should be played during the killing of the servant, in the taunting of Gloucester and when she reacts to Cornwall's wounding.

Out vile jelly! Some productions shift the blinding off-stage altogether. Other productions play the blinding in total darkness. Others heighten the agony with realistic presentations, and show Gloucester shrieking in unbearable pain. Write detailed notes on how you would stage the blinding, identifying what the audience would see. (See also page 132, Activities 1 and 2.)

If you did wear ... quarrel if you were a man, I'd fight you
stand up defy us
enkindle set alight

nature natural justice
quit punish, repay
made the overture ... us told us of your treachery

SERVANT If you did wear a beard upon your chin   75
      I'd shake it on this quarrel. What do you mean?
CORNWALL My villain!
SERVANT Nay then, come on, and take the chance of anger.
                        [They draw and fight]
REGAN *[To another Servant]* Give me thy sword. A peasant stand up
      thus!
                        Kills him
SERVANT Oh, I am slain. My lord, you have one eye left   80
      To see some mischief on him. Oh!   *[He dies]*
CORNWALL Lest it see more, prevent it. Out, vile jelly!
      [He puts out Gloucester's other eye]
      Where is thy lustre now?
GLOUCESTER All dark and comfortless. Where's my son Ed-
      mond?
      Edmond, enkindle all the sparks of nature   85
      To quit this horrid act.
REGAN   Out, treacherous villain!
      Thou call'st on him that hates thee. It was he
      That made the overture of thy treasons to us,
      Who is too good to pity thee.
GLOUCESTER O, my follies! Then Edgar was abused.   90
      Kind gods, forgive me that, and prosper him.
REGAN Go thrust him out at gates, and let him smell
      His way to Dover.
               Exit [a Servant] with Gloucester
      How is't, my lord? How look you?
CORNWALL I have received a hurt. Follow me, lady.
      [To Servants] Turn out that eyeless villain. Throw this
      slave   95
      Upon the dunghill. Regan, I bleed apace.
      Untimely comes this hurt. Give me your arm.
                      Exeunt

Looking back at Act 3
Activities for groups or individuals

1 Violence on stage

The blinding of Gloucester is often cited by those for and against show-ing violence on stage, television or film. Some argue that if Shakespeare can include horrific brutality in his plays, why can't modern script writers?

Imagine that a school or college drama club wants to mount a pro-duction of *King Lear*, but the Principal insists the blinding should be done off-stage, and not seen by the audience. Role-play a meeting between the Principal and protesting members of the production team.

2 Signs of goodness

Some hope is provided in Scene 7 in the actions of the brave servant who sacrifices himself for Gloucester. He acts as a reminder that good-ness could reign again in Lear's kingdom. In the quarto version of the play (see page 232), Scene 7 closes with two other servants who decide to assist the blinded Gloucester. They express revulsion at Cornwall and Gonerill's evil, and plan to soothe Gloucester's pain ('I'll fetch some flax and whites of eggs / To apply to his bleeding face'), and call on heaven to help him. In the theatre, the interval is often placed at the end of this scene. Decide, with reasons, whether you would include the two kind servants from the quarto version to conclude the first half of the play.

3 The Fool disappears

The Fool says and does less and less as Act 3 progresses, especially after the appearance of Poor Tom. Indeed, he disappears altogether after Scene 6. Think of reasons why Shakespeare chose to reduce the Fool's role in Act 3, and to have him play no further part in the action.

4 Why this short scene?

Scene 5, the brief conversation between Cornwall and Edmond, is sandwiched between two storm scenes, which makes staging difficult. But it must have been placed here purposely, as an integral part of the dramatic construction of the play. Suggest possible reasons for includ-ing it at this point.

5 Design the hovel

Scene 6 is played inside the hovel which sheltered Poor Tom in Scene 4. Sketch a design for the hovel showing both its outside, for Scene 4, and its inside, for Scene 6.

Suggest a suitable caption for this picture of Lear and the Fool in Scene 2.

Edgar reflects on the advantages of being destitute. He is shocked by the sight of his blinded father. In despair, Gloucester acknowledges his past errors. He regrets his treatment of Edgar.

1 At the bottom of Fortune's wheel (in pairs)

Using the image of the wheel of fortune (see page 201), Edgar reflects that pretending to be an insane beggar brings advantages. He prefers life as an outcast and the knowledge that he is despised to the illusions involved when people are admired insincerely. He feels safe as 'the low'st' on Fortune's wheel because he can hope for improvement.

Some people living as homeless beggars outside today's society share Edgar's positive attitude, and see advantages in their lifestyle. One partner reads Edgar's lines 1–9, pausing at each full stop to allow their partner to express a modern viewpoint.

2 'I stumbled when I saw'

Gloucester expresses regret at his past mistakes. As Gloucester, identify the earlier events in the play which you now feel involved stumbling and error. Write a paragraph on each of these mistakes, commenting how suffering has given you new understanding of each event.

3 A son sees his blinded father (in groups of three)

Edgar seems calm and resigned in lines 1–9, but then endures the shock of seeing his blinded father and of hearing himself lovingly described. He also has the strange experience of hearing his own feelings echoed when Gloucester says that there are advantages in suffering (lines 20–1).

Two people read lines 12–24. The third, as Edgar, uses body language to convey his response.

---

esperance hope
parti-eyed with bleeding eyes
But that except that
mutations changes
yield to age accept age and death
means goods, property

secure us give us a false sense of security
our mere defects the things we lack
commodities opportunities, advantages

Act 4 Scene 1
Near Gloucester's castle

Enter EDGAR *(disguised as a madman)*

EDGAR Yet better thus, and known to be condemned,
　　　Than still condemned and flattered. To be worst,
　　　The low'st and most dejected thing of fortune,
　　　Stands still in esperance, lives not in fear.
　　　The lamentable change is from the best;　　　　　　　　5
　　　The worst returns to laughter. Welcome, then,
　　　Thou unsubstantial air that I embrace:
　　　The wretch that thou hast blown unto the worst
　　　Owes nothing to thy blasts.

Enter GLOUCESTER *and an* OLD MAN

　　　　　　　　　　　　But who comes here?
　　　My father, parti-eyed? World, world, O world!　　　　10
　　　But that thy strange mutations make us hate thee,
　　　Life would not yield to age.
OLD MAN　　　　　　　　　O my good lord,
　　　I have been your tenant and your father's tenant
　　　These fourscore –
GLOUCESTER Away, get thee away; good friend, be gone.　　　15
　　　Thy comforts can do me no good at all;
　　　Thee they may hurt.
OLD MAN　　　　　　　You cannot see your way.
GLOUCESTER I have no way, and therefore want no eyes:
　　　I stumbled when I saw. Full oft 'tis seen,
　　　Our means secure us, and our mere defects　　　　　20
　　　Prove our commodities. Oh, dear son Edgar,
　　　The food of thy abusèd father's wrath:
　　　Might I but live to see thee in my touch,
　　　I'd say I had eyes again.
OLD MAN　　　　　　　　How now? Who's there?

Edgar fears that worse events may follow. Gloucester recalls that Poor Tom reminded him of Edgar, and reflects that humans are the playthings of the gods. He asks if Edgar knows the way to Dover.

1 Edgar's asides

In lines 1–9, Edgar took comfort in the security of being at the bottom of Fortune's wheel. Seeing and overhearing his blinded father, he finds that he was mistaken, and that his suffering is even more acute.

Edgar's five 'Asides', express his private thoughts, and are not heard by the others on stage. Decide how each aside could be spoken, and whether Edgar is addressing the audience, the gods, or speaking to himself.

2 'As flies to wanton boys' (in groups of six or more)

Edgar hears his father say that, just as irresponsible boys torment and kill flies, so human life merely provides casual entertainment for the gods. Stand or sit in a circle. One person speak Gloucester's lines 36–7, deciding whether to make them sound desperate, accepting, enraged or depressed. The next person in the circle replies with Edgar's words 'How should this be?', varying their tone of voice to suit the tone taken by the first speaker. Repeat the activity around the circle until everyone has had the opportunity to speak as both Edgar and Gloucester. Afterwards, talk together about whether you share Gloucester's opinion.

3 'Bad is the trade'

Edgar appears to decide to continue deceiving his father, in spite of his own criticism of such behaviour in lines 38–9. Do you think he is justified in choosing to 'play fool to sorrow'? Give reasons for your reply.

---

reason sense
scarce barely
wanton unthinking
twain two
ancient love old loyalty (the man's eighty-year tenancy)

time's plague curse of our times
'parel apparel (clothing)
daub it further pretend any longer

EDGAR [*Aside*] O gods! Who is't can say 'I am at the worst'?   25
    I am worse than e'er I was.
OLD MAN   'Tis poor mad Tom.
EDGAR [*Aside*] And worse I may be yet. The worst is not
    So long as we can say 'This is the worst.'
OLD MAN Fellow, where goest?
GLOUCESTER   Is it a beggarman?
OLD MAN Madman and beggar too.   30
GLOUCESTER He has some reason, else he could not beg.
    I'th'last night's storm I such a fellow saw,
    Which made me think a man a worm. My son
    Came then into my mind, and yet my mind
    Was then scarce friends with him. I have heard more
        since.   35
    As flies to wanton boys are we to th'gods;
    They kill us for their sport.
EDGAR [*Aside*]   How should this be?
    Bad is the trade that must play fool to sorrow,
    Ang'ring itself and others. – Bless thee, master.
GLOUCESTER Is that the naked fellow?
OLD MAN   Ay, my lord.   40
GLOUCESTER Get thee away. If for my sake
    Thou wilt o'ertake us hence a mile or twain
    I'th'way toward Dover, do it for ancient love,
    And bring some covering for this naked soul,
    Which I'll entreat to lead me.   45
OLD MAN Alack, sir, he is mad.
GLOUCESTER 'Tis the time's plague when madmen lead the
        blind.
    Do as I bid thee; or rather do thy pleasure.
    Above the rest, be gone.
OLD MAN I'll bring him the best 'parel that I have,   50
    Come on't what will.   *Exit*
GLOUCESTER   Sirrah, naked fellow.
EDGAR Poor Tom's a-cold. [*Aside*] I cannot daub it further.
GLOUCESTER Come hither, fellow.
EDGAR [*Aside*] And yet I must. – Bless thy sweet eyes, they bleed.
GLOUCESTER Know'st thou the way to Dover?   55

Gloucester hopes for a more just society. Edgar, as Poor Tom, agrees to guide Gloucester to Dover. Oswald tells Gonerill that Albany welcomes the French invasion, and criticises Gonerill's and Edmond's actions.

1 The naming of fiends

In the quarto version of the play (see page 232), Edgar adds, after line 58:

> Five fiends have been in poor Tom at once: of lust, as Obidicut; Hobbididence Prince of dumbness; Mahu, of stealing; Modo, of murder; Flibbertigibbet, of mopping and mowing, who since possesses chambermaids and waiting-women. So, bless thee, master!

How do you think these lines should be spoken: comically, or threateningly, or …? Give reasons for whether or not you would include the lines in your own production.

2 The blindness of wealth (in small groups)

Gloucester's blinding has brought him new insight into human problems. His traumatic experience has brought a sharp awareness of issues which he seemed happy to ignore before. He calls on the gods to punish people whose rich lifestyle 'blinds' them to the needs of others. Wealth should be redistributed fairly 'So distribution should undo excess'. Gloucester, until recently a wealthy aristocrat, appears to be suggesting a socialist solution. Talk together about the following:

a Do you agree with Gloucester that great wealth distances people from life around them and clouds their judgement? Are some people today still blinded by wealth to the needs of others?

b What do you think other characters in the play might have to say about Gloucester's suggestion that wealth should be redistributed?

---

goodman householder, yeoman
humbled to all strokes made victim of all hardships
superfluous and lust-dieted man excessively rich and lustful man
slaves your ordinance makes the law serve his own desires

confinèd deep narrow sea (the Straits of Dover)
sot fool
turned the wrong side out got things the wrong way round (by mistaking loyalty for treachery)

EDGAR Both stile and gate, horseway and footpath. Poor Tom hath
   been scared out of his good wits. Bless thee, goodman's son,
   from the foul fiend.
GLOUCESTER Here, take this purse, thou whom the heavens'
      plagues
      Have humbled to all strokes. That I am wretched   60
      Makes thee the happier. Heavens deal so still.
      Let the superfluous and lust-dieted man
      That slaves your ordinance, that will not see
      Because he does not feel, feel your power quickly.
      So distribution should undo excess,   65
      And each man have enough. Dost thou know Dover?
EDGAR Ay, master.
GLOUCESTER There is a cliff whose high and bending head
      Looks fearfully in the confinèd deep.
      Bring me but to the very brim of it,   70
      And I'll repair the misery thou dost bear
      With something rich about me. From that place
      I shall no leading need.
EDGAR   Give me thy arm.
      Poor Tom shall lead thee.
                                                              Exeunt

ACT 4   SCENE 2
A room in the castle of Gonerill and Albany

Enter GONERILL with EDMOND and OSWALD, *severally*

GONERILL Welcome, my lord. I marvel our mild husband
      Not met us on the way. – Now, where's your master?
OSWALD Madam, within; but never man so changed.
      I told him of the army that was landed;
      He smiled at it. I told him you were coming;   5
      His answer was, 'The worse'. Of Gloucester's treachery,
      And of the loyal service of his son
      When I informed him, then he called me sot,
      And told me I had turned the wrong side out.
      What most he should dislike seems pleasant to him;   10
      What like, offensive.

Gonerill criticises Albany's cowardice and bids Edmond an affectionate farewell. She reflects on how much she prefers Edmond to her husband. Albany and Gonerill exchange vicious insults.

1 'Monsters of the deep' (in pairs)

The quarto includes lines after 'Blows in your face' (line 33), which show the hostility between husband and wife:

> I fear your disposition:
> That nature which condemns its origin
> Cannot be bordered certain in itself.
> She that herself will sliver and disbranch
> From her material sap, perforce must wither
> And come to deadly use.

GONERILL   No more, the text is foolish.

ALBANY Wisdom and goodness to the vile seem vile;
> Filths savour but themselves. What have you done?
> Tigers, not daughters, what have you performed?
> A father, and a gracious agèd man,
> Whose reverence even the head-lugged bear would lick,
> Most barbarous, most degenerate, have you madded.
> Could my good brother suffer you to do it?
> A man, a prince, by him so benefited?
> If that the heavens do not their visible spirits
> Send quickly down to tame these vile offences,
> It will come.
> Humanity must perforce prey on itself
> Like monsters of the deep.

Albany likens Gonerill to a branch cut from a tree which is useful only as firewood. Regan and Gonerill's cruel treatment of Lear forecasts that humans will become like 'monsters of the deep'. (For an activity on these additional lines, see Activity 1 on page 142.)

He'll not feel ... answer he will ignore insults which demand a response
May prove effects may be fulfilled
musters gathering of soldiers
conduct his powers escort his forces
distaff stick for spinning wool

My fool usurps my body my husband undeservingly possesses me
Who hast not ... suffering you cannot see the difference between honour and disgrace
Proper natural

GONERILL [*To Edmond*] Then shall you go no further.
　　　　It is the cowish terror of his spirit
　　　　That dares not undertake. He'll not feel wrongs
　　　　Which tie him to an answer. Our wishes on the way　　　15
　　　　May prove effects. Back, Edmond, to my brother.
　　　　Hasten his musters and conduct his powers.
　　　　I must change names at home and give the distaff
　　　　Into my husband's hands. This trusty servant
　　　　Shall pass between us. Ere long you are like to hear　　　20
　　　　(If you dare venture in your own behalf)
　　　　A mistress's command. Wear this; spare speech.
　　　　Decline your head. This kiss, if it durst speak,
　　　　Would stretch thy spirits up into the air.
　　　　Conceive, and fare thee well.　　　25
EDMOND Yours in the ranks of death.
GONERILL　　　　　　　　　　　My most dear Gloucester.
　　　　　　　　　　　　　　　　Exit [*Edmond*]
　　　　Oh, the difference of man and man.
　　　　To thee a woman's services are due;
　　　　My fool usurps my body.
OSWALD Madam, here comes my lord.　　　　　　　　[*Exit*]　30

　　　　　　　　　　Enter ALBANY

GONERILL I have been worth the whistle.
ALBANY　　　　　　　　　　　O Gonerill,
　　　　You are not worth the dust which the rude wind
　　　　Blows in your face.
GONERILL　　　　　　Milk-livered man,
　　　　That bear'st a cheek for blows, a head for wrongs;
　　　　Who hast not in thy brows an eye discerning　　　35
　　　　Thine honour from thy suffering –
ALBANY　　　　　　　　　　See thyself, devil:
　　　　Proper deformity shows not in the fiend
　　　　So horrid as in woman.
GONERILL　　　　　　O vain fool!

A messenger brings news of Cornwall's death and of Gloucester's blinding. Gonerill fears Regan as a rival who could destroy her plans for a life with Edmond. Albany vows to avenge Gloucester's blinding.

1 More husband and wife hostility (in pairs)

In the quarto version of the play (see page 232), the argument between Albany and Gonerill continues. Before the messenger enters (line 38), Albany accuses Gonerill of having changed from woman into monster. He threatens her, but she replies by contemptuously mocking his manhood:

> ALBANY Thou changèd and self-covered thing, for shame
> Be-monster not thy feature. Were't my fitness
> To let these hands obey my blood,
> They are apt enough to dislocate and tear
> Thy flesh and bones. Howe'er thou art a fiend,
> A woman's shape doth shield thee.
> GONERILL Marry, your manhood! Mew!

Take roles as a director and as an actor playing Albany. The director does not wish to include these lines and the quarto lines on page 140, but Albany does. Persuade your partner that your preference has more merit.

2 Proof of the existence of the gods?

Albany reacts to the news of Cornwall's death by claiming it as proof of the existence of divine 'justicers' who punish crime in the human world. Do you see Cornwall's death as the result of action by the gods, or as the result of natural human goodness on the part of the servant who attacked him? Or would you suggest other reasons?

---

bred brought up
thrilled with remorse driven by pity
plucked him after dragged him following (to death)
justicers judges
nether earthly

my Gloucester Edmond
all the building ... hateful life demolish all my dreams of Edmond and condemn me to continued life with Albany
tart sour

Enter a MESSENGER

MESSENGER O my good lord, the Duke of Cornwall's dead,
         Slain by his servant going to put out   40
         The other eye of Gloucester.
ALBANY   Gloucester's eyes?
MESSENGER A servant that he bred, thrilled with remorse,
         Opposed against the act, bending his sword
         To his great master; who, thereat enraged,
         Flew on him and amongst them felled him dead,   45
         But not without that harmful stroke which since
         Hath plucked him after.
ALBANY   This shows you are above,
         You justicers, that these our nether crimes
         So speedily can venge. But O, poor Gloucester!
         Lost he his other eye?
MESSENGER   Both, both, my lord.   50
         This letter, madam, craves a speedy answer:
         'Tis from your sister.
GONERILL [*Aside*]   One way I like this well;
         But being widow, and my Gloucester with her,
         May all the building in my fancy pluck
         Upon my hateful life. Another way   55
         The news is not so tart. – I'll read, and answer.   *Exit*
ALBANY Where was his son when they did take his eyes?
MESSENGER Come with my lady hither.
ALBANY   He is not here.
MESSENGER No, my good lord; I met him back again.
ALBANY Knows he the wickedness?   60
MESSENGER Ay, my good lord; 'twas he informed against him
         And quit the house on purpose that their punishment
         Might have the freer course.
ALBANY   Gloucester, I live
         To thank thee for the love thou showed'st the king,
         And to revenge thine eyes. – Come hither, friend.   65
         Tell me what more thou know'st.
                                              Exeunt

Cordelia grieves for Lear's madness. She sends soldiers to search for Lear, who has wandered off wearing a crown of wild flowers. The Gentleman says Lear's sanity can be restored by rest.

1 An additional scene

The quarto includes an extra scene after the end of Scene 2. You can find it on pages 234–5.

Cordelia returns to Britain at the head of the invading French army. The language used by Cordelia and the Gentleman echoes the richness and the healing power of nature ('aidant and remediate'). Do you think that having Cordelia dressed as a soldier strengthens or weakens the imagery of the restorative powers of nature? In some productions, she appears dressed in armour from head to foot. Suggest how she would be costumed in your own production of the play.

---

colours military flags
furrow-weeds weeds growing in ploughed land
fumitor ... Darnel various weeds
century hundred soldiers
What ... wisdom what can knowledge achieve

bereavèd impaired, lost
simples operative effective medicinal herbs
unpublished virtues secret strengths (herbs)
wants the means to lead it lacks reason to control his rage

ACT 4 SCENE 3
The French camp near Dover

Enter with drum and colours, CORDELIA, GENTLEMAN
and Soldiers

CORDELIA Alack, 'tis he: why, he was met even now,
    As mad as the vexed sea, singing aloud,
    Crowned with rank fumitor and furrow-weeds,
    With burdocks, hemlock, nettles, cuckoo-flowers,
    Darnel, and all the idle weeds that grow   5
    In our sustaining corn. A century send forth.
    Search every acre in the high-grown field,
    And bring him to our eye.
                        [Exit an Officer]
              What can man's wisdom
    In the restoring his bereavèd sense?
    He that helps him take all my outward worth.   10
GENTLEMAN There is means, madam.
    Our foster-nurse of nature is repose,
    The which he lacks. That to provoke in him
    Are many simples operative, whose power
    Will close the eye of anguish.
CORDELIA   All blest secrets,   15
    All you unpublished virtues of the earth,
    Spring with my tears; be aidant and remediate
    In the good man's distress. – Seek, seek for him,
    Lest his ungoverned rage dissolve the life
    That wants the means to lead it.

Enter MESSENGER

MESSENGER   News, madam.   20
    The British powers are marching hitherward.

Cordelia declares that love, not political ambition, makes her fight. In Scene 4, Regan questions Oswald closely, and says that Edmond has gone in search of Gloucester in order to kill him.

1 Cordelia's motivation (in small groups)

Cordelia claims that she is leading an invading French army to Britain, not out of a desire for power, but in order to rescue and support her father. Her lines 23–4 echo words spoken by Jesus in the New Testament (Luke 2:49). This has led some people to see her as a Christ-like figure, one capable of great self-sacrifice in order to redeem and to relieve suffering.

To help you decide to whom Cordelia is making her declaration, try speaking lines 23–9 in different ways. For example, as though she were:

- calling out to her lost father
- kneeling in prayer to the gods
- weeping and explaining the situation to the Gentleman
- speaking in some other way.

Decide which way of speaking the lines you think would be the most effective on stage.

2 Albany's dilemma

Cordelia brings a French army to Britain to help her father. Her action has put Albany in a difficult situation, torn between loyalty to his king and the wish to defend Britain from a foreign invasion. Such divided loyalties may account for Albany's reluctance ('much ado', line 4) to go to war. Draw a sketch of Albany trying to decide on his course of action. Draw speech bubbles all around your Albany figure, each one containing a few words about one of the many different pressures and ideas which are influencing him as he decides what to do.

---

importuned persistent, beseeching
No blown … incite we don't fight because of puffed-up ambition
brother's powers Albany's army
import signify, mean

posted hence ridden away speedily
ignorance foolishness
'nighted benighted (ignorant) or blinded (plunged into darkness)
descry establish, find out

CORDELIA 'Tis known before. Our preparation stands
     In expectation of them. – O dear father,
     It is thy business that I go about:
     Therefore great France   25
     My mourning and importuned tears hath pitied.
     No blown ambition doth our arms incite,
     But love, dear love, and our aged father's right.
     Soon may I hear and see him.

Exeunt

ACT 4   SCENE 4
A room in Gloucester's castle

Enter REGAN *and* OSWALD

REGAN But are my brother's powers set forth?
OSWALD Ay, madam.
REGAN Himself in person there?
OSWALD Madam, with much ado.
     Your sister is the better soldier.   5
REGAN Lord Edmond spake not with your lord at home?
OSWALD No, madam.
REGAN What might import my sister's letter to him?
OSWALD I know not, lady.
REGAN Faith, he is posted hence on serious matter.   10
     It was great ignorance, Gloucester's eyes being out,
     To let him live. Where he arrives he moves
     All hearts against us. Edmond, I think, is gone,
     In pity of his misery, to dispatch
     His 'nighted life, moreover to descry   15
     The strength o'th'enemy.
OSWALD I must needs after him, madam, with my letter.
REGAN Our troops set forth tomorrow. Stay with us.
     The ways are dangerous.
OSWALD   I may not, madam.
     My lady charged my duty in this business.   20

Regan urges Oswald to give her Gonerill's letter, and claims that she should be Edmond's partner. She offers to reward anyone who kills Gloucester. Edgar deceives Gloucester into believing that they are climbing a slope.

1 Directing decisions (in pairs)

Scene 4 can be performed in very different ways on stage. Actors need to decide:

- how to play lines 21–4, in which Regan appears to keep changing her mind
- whether or not Regan opens and reads the letter (lines 24–5)
- whether 'note' in line 31 refers to a letter or means 'note this carefully'
- what it is that Oswald 'may gather more' of (line 34)
- what Regan gives Oswald at line 35.

Act out lines 21–42 in a way which makes clear your decision on each of these issues.

2 'Strange oeilliads' (in pairs)

Show your partner the 'strange oeilliads and most speaking looks' that Gonerill gave Edmond (line 27).

3 'Look how we labour'

In lines 1–6, Edgar tries to convince his father that they are climbing a hill. What advice would you give the actor playing Edgar? Bear in mind that his father's blindness means that Edgar does not have to prevent his real feelings from showing.

---

oeilliads significant glances
of her bosom in her confidence
call her wisdom to her to act with
  good sense

Preferment promotion
cuts him off kills him

REGAN Why should she write to Edmond? Might not you
     Transport her purposes by word? Belike –
     Some things – I know not what. I'll love thee much:
     Let me unseal the letter.
OSWALD   Madam, I had rather –
REGAN I know your lady does not love her husband.   25
     I am sure of that; and at her late being here
     She gave strange oeilliads and most speaking looks
     To noble Edmond. I know you are of her bosom.
OSWALD I, madam?
REGAN I speak in understanding. Y'are, I know't.   30
     Therefore I do advise you take this note:
     My lord is dead; Edmond and I have talked;
     And more convenient is he for my hand
     Than for your lady's. You may gather more.
     If you do find him, pray you give him this;   35
     And when your mistress hears thus much from you,
     I pray desire her call her wisdom to her.
     So, fare you well.
     If you do chance to hear of that blind traitor,
     Preferment falls on him that cuts him off.   40
OSWALD Would I could meet him, madam, I should show
     What party I do follow.
REGAN   Fare thee well.   *Exeunt*

ACT 4   SCENE 5
The countryside near Dover

Enter GLOUCESTER and EDGAR (dressed like a peasant)

GLOUCESTER When shall I come to th'top of that same hill?
EDGAR You do climb up it now. Look how we labour.
GLOUCESTER Methinks the ground is even.
EDGAR   Horrible steep.
     Hark, do you hear the sea?
GLOUCESTER   No, truly.
EDGAR Why, then your other senses grow imperfect   5
     By your eyes' anguish.

Edgar describes the alarming view which he claims to see. Gloucester asks to be set at the very edge of the cliff. Edgar says that he is misleading his father in order to save him from despair.

1 Creating an imaginary view (in pairs)

a Edgar has deceived his father into believing they have climbed the steep slope leading to the cliff edge at Dover. To convince him they are at the very edge, he describes the view from the clifftop. Practise speaking lines 11–24 as persuasively as possible.

b Edgar describes the noise of the waves in lines 20–1 ('the murmuring surge … chafes'). His words suggest the sound of the sea. Using words which echo their meaning in their sound is called onomatopoeia. Try saying the lines aloud to express how the tide shifts pebbles at the sea's edge.

2 Why does Edgar lie?

When Edgar first began to deceive his blinded father he said, 'Bad is the trade that must play fool to sorrow' (Act 4 Scene 1, line 38), apparently regretting the unpleasant necessity of playing the fool to someone so vulnerable and distressed. Now Edgar tells an elaborate sequence of lies about what he can see. In lines 33–4, he states his motive for misleading his father, perhaps to reassure the audience as well as himself. How do you respond to Edgar's behaviour?

---

phrase and matter style and content
choughs type of crow (pronounced 'chuffs')
samphire an edible plant
barque ship

cock small boat towed behind a larger one
For all beneath the moon for the whole world
Prosper it increase it (fairies were believed to increase hidden treasure)

GLOUCESTER   So may it be indeed.
   Methinks thy voice is altered, and thou speak'st
   In better phrase and matter than thou didst.
EDGAR Y'are much deceived. In nothing am I changed
   But in my garments.
GLOUCESTER   Methinks y'are better spoken.   10
EDGAR Come on, sir, here's the place. Stand still. How fearful
   And dizzy 'tis to cast one's eyes so low.
   The crows and choughs that wing the midway air
   Show scarce so gross as beetles. Half-way down
   Hangs one that gathers samphire, dreadful trade!   15
   Methinks he seems no bigger than his head.
   The fishermen that walk upon the beach
   Appear like mice, and yon tall anchoring barque
   Diminished to her cock; her cock, a buoy
   Almost too small for sight. The murmuring surge,   20
   That on th'unnumbered idle pebble chafes,
   Cannot be heard so high. I'll look no more,
   Lest my brain turn and the deficient sight
   Topple down headlong.
GLOUCESTER   Set me where you stand.
EDGAR Give me your hand. You are now within a foot   25
   Of th'extreme verge. For all beneath the moon
   Would I not leap upright.
GLOUCESTER   Let go my hand.
   Here, friend, 's another purse: in it, a jewel
   Well worth a poor man's taking. Fairies and gods
   Prosper it with thee. Go thou further off.   30
   Bid me farewell, and let me hear thee going.
EDGAR Now fare ye well, good sir.
GLOUCESTER   With all my heart.
EDGAR [*Aside*] Why I do trifle thus with his despair
   Is done to cure it.

Gloucester tells the gods that he intends to kill himself. He throws himself forward. Edgar pretends to be someone standing on the beach who saw him fall and land in safety. Gloucester is confused and distressed.

1 Defiance, patience or despair? (in pairs)

Gloucester is determined to kill himself. In Shakespeare's time, Christians saw suicide as a terrible, unforgivable sin against God. Those who committed suicide were denied Christian burial. Gloucester tells the gods that, even if he continued to endure life ('bear it longer') and did not challenge the destiny the gods have decreed for him ('great opposeless wills'), his exhausted body would die like a burnt out candle.

Practise speaking Gloucester's lines 34–40 in different ways, to discover a version which you think would be appropriate on stage. For example:

- despairingly, emphasising his helplessness
- defiantly, emphasising his feeling of being in control
- patiently, emphasising his humility.

2 Comedy, tragedy, absurdity?

Audiences sometimes laugh at Gloucester's fall over an imaginary cliff on a flat stage. His action can seem comic and absurd. If you were directing the play, how would you want the audience to respond?

3 Edgar – manipulator or rescuer?

Many people find it painful to watch a performance of this scene because Gloucester's suffering is intense and because he is being manipulated by his son. Advise the actor playing Edgar how he could deliver each speech in lines 41–80.

---

opposeless irresistable
snuff smouldering candle-end (old age)
conceit imagination
pass die
aught but gossamer anything but fine silk

shivered shattered
perpendicularly straight down
bourn boundary (Dover cliff)
shrill-gorged shrill-throated
beguile ... his proud will cheat the fury of a dictator and disobey his wishes (by suicide)

GLOUCESTER [*Kneels*]   O you mighty gods!
  This world I do renounce, and in your sights   35
  Shake patiently my great affliction off.
  If I could bear it longer and not fall
  To quarrel with your great opposeless wills,
  My snuff and loathèd part of nature should
  Burn itself out. If Edgar live, O bless him.   40
  Now, fellow, fare thee well.
EDGAR   Gone, sir; farewell.
        [*Gloucester throws himself forward and falls*]
  [*Aside*] And yet I know not how conceit may rob
  The treasury of life, when life itself
  Yields to the theft. Had he been where he thought,
  By this had thought been past. – Alive or dead?   45
  Ho, you sir, friend! Hear you, sir? Speak!
  [*Aside*] Thus might he pass indeed. Yet he revives. –
  What are you, sir?
GLOUCESTER   Away, and let me die.
EDGAR Hadst thou been aught but gossamer, feathers, air,
  So many fathom down precipitating,   50
  Thou'dst shivered like an egg. But thou dost breathe,
  Hast heavy substance, bleed'st not, speak'st, art sound.
  Ten masts at each make not the altitude
  Which thou hast perpendicularly fell.
  Thy life's a miracle. Speak yet again.   55
GLOUCESTER But have I fall'n or no?
EDGAR From the dread summit of this chalky bourn.
  Look up a-height: the shrill-gorged lark so far
  Cannot be seen or heard; do but look up.
GLOUCESTER Alack, I have no eyes.   60
  Is wretchedness deprived that benefit
  To end itself by death? 'Twas yet some comfort
  When misery could beguile the tyrant's rage
  And frustrate his proud will.
EDGAR   Give me your arm.
  Up; so. How is't? Feel you your legs? You stand.   65
GLOUCESTER Too well, too well.

Gloucester determines to endure his suffering. Edgar urges him to feel free of guilt. Lear's disordered talk is of archers, mice and challenges. He acknowledges that flatterers misled him.

'*Enter* LEAR, [*mad*].' Lear's strange language may have some kind of sense. In lines 85–90, he talks of money paid to recently enlisted troops ('press-money'); orders an archer to stretch his bow to its full extent ('Draw me a clothier's yard'), imitates the whistling noise of an arrow ('Hewgh!'); and imagines it hitting the centre of the target ('i'th'clout').

---

whelked twisted
make them honours / Of men's impossibilities gain reverence by performing miracles
The safer ... master thus a sane mind would never allow its owner to dress like this

side-piercing heart-breaking
marjoram a herb (with healing properties)
no good divinity bad theology
ague-proof immune to fevers

EDGAR   This is above all strangeness.
        Upon the crown o'th'cliff what thing was that
        Which parted from you?
GLOUCESTER   A poor unfortunate beggar.
EDGAR As I stood here below, methought his eyes
        Were two full moons. He had a thousand noses,   70
        Horns whelked and waved like the enragèd sea.
        It was some fiend. Therefore, thou happy father,
        Think that the clearest gods, who make them honours
        Of men's impossibilities, have preserved thee.
GLOUCESTER I do remember now. Henceforth I'll bear   75
        Affliction till it do cry out itself
        'Enough, enough', and die. That thing you speak of,
        I took it for a man. Often 'twould say
        'The fiend, the fiend!' He led me to that place.
EDGAR Bear free and patient thoughts.

                    Enter LEAR, [*mad*]

                    But who comes here?   80
        The safer sense will ne'er accommodate
        His master thus.
LEAR No, they cannot touch me for crying. I am the king himself.
EDGAR O thou side-piercing sight!
LEAR Nature's above art in that respect. There's your press-   85
        money. That fellow handles his bow like a crow-keeper. Draw
        me a clothier's yard. Look, look, a mouse! Peace, peace, this
        piece of toasted cheese will do't. There's my gauntlet. I'll prove
        it on a giant. Bring up the brown bills. O well flown bird:
        i'th'clout, i'th'clout! Hewgh! Give the word.   90
EDGAR Sweet marjoram.
LEAR Pass.
GLOUCESTER I know that voice.
LEAR Ha! Gonerill with a white beard? They flattered me like a
        dog and told me I had the white hairs in my beard ere the black   95
        ones were there. To say 'ay' and 'no' to everything that I said
        'ay' and 'no' to was no good divinity. When the rain came to
        wet me once and the wind to make me chatter, when the
        thunder would not peace at my bidding, there I found 'em,
        there I smelt 'em out. Go to, they are not men o'their words.   100
        They told me I was everything; 'tis a lie, I am not ague-proof.

*Gloucester recognises the king's voice. Lear embarks on a frenzied
condemnation of women's sexuality. Gloucester asks whether Lear recognises
him. The king seems to mock Gloucester's empty eye sockets.*

1 The language of sexual disgust (in small groups)

Lear's language reflects the disturbance and distress of his mind. He
shows an obsessive interest in sex, and an intense fear and loathing of
women's sexual desires. He sees evidence of sexuality all around him:
'lecher' = copulate, 'luxury' = lust, 'fitchew' = a polecat (a slang term
for a prostitute), 'soilèd' = oversexed, 'centaurs' = legendary creatures
(half horse, half human).

Try different ways of speaking lines 103–27 to bring out Lear's initial
haughtiness followed by his deep sexual loathing. Afterwards, talk
together about each of the following:

a What does Lear's sexual disgust suggest about his character?

b How do you think each of Lear's three daughters would react if they
could hear their father's words?

c Which significant themes in the play might Lear's words echo?

d Write some advice to an actor on how to deliver the lines.

e Find a copy of Shakespeare's sonnet 129, and compare its language
and tone with Lear's lines.

2 'It smells of mortality'

Gloucester chooses to show Lear the courtesy due to a king by wanting
to kiss his hand. Lear's response emphasises his humanity rather than
his royalty. But does he accept Gloucester's request?

---

cause offence
pell-mell promiscuously, riotously
face between ... presages snow
 face predicts that she will be
 sexually frigid ('forks' = legs)
minces pretends to prefer
girdle waist

inherit possess
civet perfume
Shall so wear out to naught will
 similarly decay to nothing
squiny squint
challenge summons to a duel
take believe

GLOUCESTER The trick of that voice I do well remember.
          Is't not the king?
LEAR   Ay, every inch a king.
          When I do stare, see how the subject quakes.
          I pardon that man's life. What was thy cause?   105
          Adultery?
          Thou shalt not die. Die for adultery? No,
          The wren goes to't, and the small gilded fly
          Does lecher in my sight.
          Let copulation thrive: for Gloucester's bastard son   110
          Was kinder to his father than my daughters
          Got 'tween the lawful sheets.
          To't, luxury, pell-mell, for I lack soldiers.
          Behold yon simp'ring dame,
          Whose face between her forks presages snow,   115
          That minces virtue, and does shake the head
          To hear of pleasure's name.
          The fitchew nor the soilèd horse goes to't
          With a more riotous appetite.
          Down from the waist they're centaurs,   120
          Though women all above.
          But to the girdle do the gods inherit;
          Beneath is all the fiend's.
There's hell, there's darkness, there is the sulphurous pit,
burning, scalding, stench, consumption. Fie, fie, fie; pah, pah!   125
Give me an ounce of civet, good apothecary, sweeten my
imagination: there's money for thee.
GLOUCESTER O, let me kiss that hand!
LEAR Let me wipe it first; it smells of mortality.
GLOUCESTER O ruined piece of nature! This great world   130
          Shall so wear out to naught. Dost thou know me?
LEAR I remember thine eyes well enough. Dost thou squiny at me?
          No, do thy worst, blind Cupid, I'll not love.
          Read thou this challenge; mark but the penning of it.
GLOUCESTER Were all thy letters suns, I could not see.   135
EDGAR [Aside] I would not take this from report; it is,
          And my heart breaks at it.

Lear condemns the hypocritical and distorted justice exercised by those with power but without morality. He complains that the rich can escape punishment while the poor cannot. Lear recognises Gloucester.

1 Seeing without eyes (in pairs)

Lear seems to taunt Gloucester with his blindness, ordering him to read and using the words 'eyes', 'look' and 'see' repeatedly in lines 138–48. In response to Lear's 'you see how this world goes', Gloucester replies 'I see it feelingly'. He both 'sees' the world by touch and, because of his suffering, understands its injustices more fully than before. He has learned by bitter experience. Talk together about whether or not you believe that it is only through personal suffering that someone can really understand the unhappiness of others.

2 The great image of authority

Lear says that the image of a dog chasing off a beggar is symbolic of authority: anyone will be obeyed if they hold a position of power, irrespective of their personal worth or merit. How far do you agree with Lear's claim?

3 Double standards (in small groups)

Lear condemns hypocrisy and gives examples of hypocritical behaviour: a beadle whipping a prostitute while wishing he were one of her clients; a powerful money-lender having a minor cheat executed for lesser crimes than his own; and the fact that the sinful rich are protected from justice by their wealth, while the sinful poor are vulnerable.

Read lines 150–65 several times, changing speaker at the end of each sentence. Experiment with different ways of speaking to reflect Lear's possible moods, for example anger, affection, sulking. Consider at which points his mood may alter.

---

case of eyes empty eye sockets
rails upon criticises
handy-dandy make a guess
beadle parish officer
usurer money-lender
cozener cheat

pygmy's straw tiny, weak weapon
I'll able 'em I'll support them
scurvy vile, scheming
matter and impertinency sense
and nonsense
wawl wail

LEAR Read.

GLOUCESTER What – with the case of eyes?

LEAR O ho, are you there with me? No eyes in your head, nor no   140
money in your purse? Your eyes are in a heavy case, your purse
in a light; yet you see how this world goes.

GLOUCESTER I see it feelingly.

LEAR What, art mad? A man may see how this world goes with no
eyes; look with thine ears. See how yon justice rails upon yon   145
simple thief. Hark in thine ear: change places, and handy-
dandy, which is the justice, which is the thief? Thou hast seen
a farmer's dog bark at a beggar?

GLOUCESTER Ay, sir.

LEAR And the creature run from the cur? There thou mightst   150
behold the great image of authority. A dog's obeyed in office.
     Thou rascal beadle, hold thy bloody hand.
     Why dost thou lash that whore? Strip thy own back.
     Thou hotly lusts to use her in that kind
     For which thou whip'st her. The usurer hangs the coz-
          ener.   155
     Through tattered clothes great vices do appear:
     Robes and furred gowns hide all. Plate sin with gold,
     And the strong lance of justice hurtless breaks;
     Arm it in rags, a pygmy's straw does pierce it.
     None does offend, none, I say none. I'll able 'em.   160
     Take that of me, my friend, who have the power
     To seal th'accuser's lips. Get thee glass eyes,
     And, like a scurvy politician, seem
     To see the things thou dost not. Now, now, now, now.
     Pull off my boots. Harder, harder! So.   165

EDGAR [Aside] O matter and impertinency mixed,
     Reason in madness.

LEAR If thou wilt weep my fortunes, take my eyes.
     I know thee well enough; thy name is Gloucester.
     Thou must be patient. We came crying hither.   170
     Thou know'st the first time that we smell the air
     We wawl and cry. I will preach to thee: mark.

GLOUCESTER Alack, alack the day.

Lear imagines revenge on his enemies. He greets the search party enigmatically, then runs away. Edgar learns that the French and British armies will soon meet in battle.

1 Stage of fools (in pairs)

Lear's description of the world as 'this great stage of fools' (line 175) is echoed in other plays by Shakespeare, for example *As You Like It* (Act 2 Scene 7, line 139) and *Macbeth* (Act 5 Scene 5, lines 17–27). Brainstorm as many reasons as you can for comparing human life or the world to a stage and to explain why Lear uses the image at this moment.

2 The mysterious block (in small groups)

No one really knows the meaning of the 'good block' mentioned in line 175. It could be Lear's hat, a crown of flowers, a hat worn by Edgar or Gloucester, a mounting-block, a tree stump, a quintain (a post set up for jousting practice), or just an example of Lear's raving. Decide, with reasons, which you prefer, or make your own suggestions.

3 Catching the king

Lear manages to elude the Attendants. Suggest what motivates him to run away, then work out how his escape might be staged. Remember that he is old and frail, and that the Attendants are probably very fit soldiers.

---

delicate stratagem cunning plan
put't in proof test it
natural fool born idiot
seconds servants
man of salt man of tears
Sa, sa, sa, sa! a hunting cry
nature human nature

twain two (i.e. Gonerill and Regan)
sure and vulgar certain and widely known
the main descry ... hourly thought we expect to see the main body of the army at any time

LEAR When we are born, we cry that we are come
    To this great stage of fools. This' a good block.   175
    It were a delicate stratagem to shoe
    A troop of horse with felt. I'll put't in proof,
    And when I have stol'n upon these son-in-laws,
    Then kill, kill, kill, kill, kill, kill!

                Enter a GENTLEMAN [*with Attendants*]

GENTLEMAN O here he is: lay hand upon him. Sir,   180
    Your most dear daughter –
LEAR No rescue? What, a prisoner? I am even
    The natural fool of fortune. Use me well.
    You shall have ransom. Let me have surgeons,
    I am cut to th'brains.
GENTLEMAN   You shall have anything.   185
LEAR No seconds? All myself?
    Why, this would make a man a man of salt,
    To use his eyes for garden water-pots.
    I will die bravely, like a smug bridegroom. What?
    I will be jovial. Come, come, I am a king.   190
    Masters, know you that?
GENTLEMAN You are a royal one, and we obey you.
LEAR Then there's life in't. Come, an you get it, you shall get it by
    running. Sa, sa, sa, sa!
                                Exit [*running, Attendants following*]
GENTLEMAN A sight most pitiful in the meanest wretch,   195
    Past speaking of in a king. Thou hast a daughter
    Who redeems nature from the general curse
    Which twain have brought her to.
EDGAR   Hail, gentle sir.
GENTLEMAN Sir, speed you: what's your will?
EDGAR Do you hear aught, sir, of a battle toward?   200
GENTLEMAN Most sure and vulgar: everyone hears that,
    Which can distinguish sound.
EDGAR   But, by your favour,
    How near's the other army?
GENTLEMAN Near and on speedy foot: the main descry
    Stands on the hourly thought.
EDGAR   I thank you, sir. That's all.   205

Gloucester says that he is no longer suicidal. Edgar, expressing pity, offers to lead him to shelter. Oswald plans to kill Gloucester for the reward. Edgar, speaking as a peasant, defies Oswald. They fight.

1 'Known and feeling sorrows'

Gloucester has suffered and learned much. In lines 212–14, Edgar describes himself (in words which could apply equally to his father) as someone who through his sorrows has learned the lesson of pity. Think back over the play so far and recall the different 'sorrows' which have 'educated' Edgar and his father.

2 'Father' (in pairs)

Edgar calls Gloucester 'father', as he did earlier at line 72. 'Father' could simply mean 'old man', but Edgar may intend it quite literally, wanting to be recognised. Try out different ways of saying lines 210–11. Should the actor playing Gloucester make line 211 suggest hazy recognition of his son?

3 Oswald, brave killer of blind old men? (in groups of four)

Read Oswald's lines 217–21 and 222–5 around the group, changing speaker at each punctuation mark. Which words could be emphasised to highlight Oswald's gloating, threatening, confident behaviour?

4 A voice in disguise

Edgar adopts a country accent to challenge Oswald. You may find his words easier to understand if you speak them aloud ('chill' = I will, 'gait' = way, 'chud' = I should, 'zwaggered' = boasted, 'che vor'ye' = I tell you, 'costard' = head, 'ballow' = staff, 'foins' = sword strokes).

---

special cause particular mission
the art … sorrows the teaching of
  painfully experienced sorrows
Am pregnant to good pity have
  learned to pity
biding safe place

bounty generosity
benison blessing
To boot, and boot may also greatly
  profit you
Briefly thyself remember prepare
  yourself for death

GENTLEMAN Though that the queen on special cause is here,
    Her army is moved on.
EDGAR   I thank you, sir.

                      Exit [Gentleman]
GLOUCESTER You ever gentle gods, take my breath from me.
    Let not my worser spirit tempt me again
    To die before you please.
EDGAR   Well pray you, father.   210
GLOUCESTER Now, good sir, what are you?
EDGAR A most poor man, made tame to fortune's blows,
    Who by the art of known and feeling sorrows
    Am pregnant to good pity. Give me your hand;
    I'll lead you to some biding.
GLOUCESTER   Hearty thanks;   215
    The bounty and the benison of heaven
    To boot, and boot.

          Enter OSWALD

OSWALD   A proclaimed prize! most happy!
    That eyeless head of thine was first framed flesh
    To raise my fortunes. Thou old, unhappy traitor,
    Briefly thyself remember: the sword is out   220
    That must destroy thee.
GLOUCESTER   Now let thy friendly hand
    Put strength enough to't.
OSWALD   Wherefore, bold peasant,
    Dar'st thou support a published traitor? Hence,
    Lest that th'infection of his fortune take
    Like hold on thee. Let go his arm.   225
EDGAR Chill not let go, zir, without vurther 'casion.
OSWALD Let go slave, or thou di'st.
EDGAR Good gentleman, go your gait, and let poor volk pass. And
    chud ha' been zwaggered out of my life, 'twould not ha' been
    zo long as 'tis by a vortnight. Nay, come not near th'old man.   230
    Keep out, che vor'ye, or I s' try whether your costard or my
    ballow be the harder; chill be plain with you.
OSWALD Out, dunghill!

          [They fight]
EDGAR Chill pick your teeth, zir: come, no matter vor your foins.

Oswald, mortally wounded, asks Edgar to deliver his letters to Edmond.
Edgar reads a letter from Gonerill urging Edmond to kill Albany and marry
her. Edgar plans to take the letter to Albany.

1 'O untimely death' (in pairs)

Oswald believes that he will easily overcome an untrained peasant.
Edgar has to fight armed only with a staff. Oswald is often shown on
stage to be startled by the ferocity and skill with which Edgar fights. In
one production, Edgar felled Oswald and then repeatedly pounded
Oswald's eyes with his staff, as if avenging his father's blinding. Plan
how to stage their fight in order to show Oswald's over-confidence and
Edgar's attitude to violence. How should Oswald speak his final lines
235–9: with nobility, or bitterness, or in some other way?

2 'A serviceable villain'

Edgar describes Oswald as a 'serviceable villain', someone who fawns,
flatters and makes themselves useful. Decide whether or not you think
'serviceable villain' is an apt description of Oswald. (See Activity 3, page
124.)

3 'To know our enemies' minds' (in pairs)

Until Edgar reads the letter, he has no knowledge of his brother's relationship with Gonerill. To help you understand how Edgar explores the
meanings and tone of the letter, stand back to back. One person reads
the whole letter in a matter-of-fact, unemotional way. The other then
reads it in a way which emphasises all the suggestions of a conspiracy
and an intimate relationship.

---

deathsman executioner
Leave by your leave, pardon
gentle wax seal on letter
reciprocal jointly sworn
for your labour as a reward for your
  efforts, for your sexual exertion
indistinguished indefinable,
  puzzling, limitless

rake up bury
post unsanctified unholy
  messenger
ungracious paper wicked letter
strike blast
death-practised duke intended
  victim of assassination

OSWALD Slave, thou hast slain me. Villain, take my purse.   235
       If ever thou wilt thrive, bury my body,
       And give the letters which thou find'st about me
       To Edmond, Earl of Gloucester: seek him out
       Upon the English party. O untimely death, death.
                                       [He dies]

EDGAR I know thee well – a serviceable villain,   240
       As duteous to the vices of thy mistress
       As badness would desire.
GLOUCESTER   What, is he dead?
EDGAR Sit you down, father; rest you.
       Let's see these pockets. The letters that he speaks of
       May be my friends. He's dead. I am only sorry   245
       He had no other deathsman. Let us see.
       Leave, gentle wax; and manners, blame us not:
       To know our enemies' minds, we rip their hearts;
       Their papers is more lawful.
                        Reads the letter

'Let our reciprocal vows be remembered. You have many   250
opportunities to cut him off. If your will want not, time and
place will be fruitfully offered. There is nothing done, if he
return the conqueror; then am I the prisoner, and his bed my
gaol, from the loathed warmth whereof, deliver me, and supply
the place for your labour.   255
               Your (wife, so I would say)
                   affectionate servant,
                            Gonerill.'

       O indistinguished space of woman's will,
       A plot upon her virtuous husband's life –   260
       And the exchange my brother! Here in the sands
       Thee I'll rake up, the post unsanctified
       Of murderous lechers; and in the mature time
       With this ungracious paper strike the sight
       Of the death-practised duke. For him 'tis well   265
       That of thy death and business I can tell.
                 [Exit, dragging out the body]

Gloucester wishes he were insane and could forget his griefs. Edgar plans to take him to safety. Cordelia thanks Kent for his loyalty. She prays that the sleeping Lear will wake to sanity.

1 'Lear's servant' and the queen

Kent and Cordelia have not met since Act 1 Scene 1, and now they meet again under very different circumstances. Cordelia is the Queen of France. Kent, although recognised by Cordelia, is disguised as Lear's servant, Caius.

Despite Cordelia's pleading ('Be better suited…'), Kent refuses to remove his disguise ('weeds' = clothes), because it would interfere with his 'made intent'. What do you think Kent is planning? Suggest why he chooses to remain in disguise.

2 Appealing to the gods (in pairs)

Cordelia compares Lear's state of mind to an untuned and discordant musical instrument. Her image is full of hope, since it suggests that recovery is possible, just as an ill-tuned instrument can be tuned back into harmony. She prays for the healing of the 'breach' in Lear's nature which will bring about his recovery.

Prayer in almost all religions is accompanied by ritualised movements, such as kneeling, pressing hands together or bowing. Devise a suitable ritual for Cordelia's prayer (lines 14–17). One partner reads the prayer while the other performs the invented ritual. Would you recommend a ritual to accompany the words in a stage production?

---

ingenious acute
wrong imaginations madness
every measure all ways of
  measuring (Kent's goodness)
modest truth simple accuracy
Nor more, nor clipped neither
  exaggerated nor understated

shortens my made intent
  interferes with my plans
boon request, favour
breach wound
Th'untuned and jarring senses
  O wind up restore to harmony his
  discordant emotions

GLOUCESTER The king is mad. How stiff is my vile sense,
That I stand up and have ingenious feeling
Of my huge sorrows! Better I were distract,
So should my thoughts be severed from my griefs,   270
                    Drum afar off
And woes by wrong imaginations lose
The knowledge of themselves.

                    [*Enter* EDGAR]

EDGAR   Give me your hand.
Far off methinks I hear the beaten drum.
Come, father, I'll bestow you with a friend.

                                                Exeunt

ACT 4   SCENE 6
The French camp near Dover

Enter CORDELIA, KENT (disguised) and GENTLEMAN

CORDELIA O thou good Kent, how shall I live and work
To match thy goodness? My life will be too short,
And every measure fail me.
KENT To be acknowledged, madam, is o'erpaid.
All my reports go with the modest truth,   5
Nor more, nor clipped, but so.
CORDELIA   Be better suited:
These weeds are memories of those worser hours.
I prithee, put them off.
KENT   Pardon, dear madam.
Yet to be known shortens my made intent.
My boon I make it that you know me not   10
Till time and I think meet.
CORDELIA Then be't so, my good lord. – How does the king?
GENTLEMAN Madam, sleeps still.
CORDELIA O you kind gods,
Cure this great breach in his abusèd nature;   15
Th'untuned and jarring senses O wind up
Of this child-changèd father!

The sleeping Lear is carried on stage, dressed in fresh clothes. Cordelia speaks of him with pity and love. On waking, Lear thinks that he may be dead and that Cordelia is an angel.

1 'Speak to him'

Relatives of people recovering from long periods of unconsciousness are urged to remind the patient constantly of who they are and that they are loved, by touching them and talking to them. Read through all Cordelia says in lines 26–47, and think about which lines are directed to Lear, and which may be spoken to others. Suggest how Cordelia speaks and behaves at each line.

2 A wheel of fire (in pairs)

Lines 42–5 are Lear's first words after his long ordeal of mental suffering. He speaks as if he were dead and suffering torment, using imagery which recalls Christian ideas about heaven, hell and the afterlife. Experiment with different ways of speaking the lines.

3 Music and additional lines

In the quarto version of the play, music is played as Cordelia speaks to Lear, and she is given four additional lines after line 32:

> To stand against the deep dread-bolted thunder?
> In the most terrible and nimble stroke
> Of quick cross lightning? to watch, poor perdu,
> With this thin helm?

Imagine that you are directing the play. Decide, with reasons, whether or not you would include music and these lines in your production ('perdu' = lost one, 'thin helm' = uncovered head).

I'th'sway of your own will as you think best
arrayed formally clothed
temperance self-control, sanity
white flakes white hairs

challenge demand
fain pleased
hovel thee stay in a dirty hut
far wide wide of the mark (still mad)

GENTLEMAN So please your majesty,
    That we may wake the king? He hath slept long.
CORDELIA Be governed by your knowledge, and proceed   20
    I'th'sway of your own will. Is he arrayed?

Enter LEAR *[asleep] in a chair carried by servants*

GENTLEMAN Ay, madam: in the heaviness of sleep
    We put fresh garments on him.
    Be by, good madam, when we do awake him;
    I doubt not of his temperance.   25
CORDELIA O my dear father, restoration hang
    Thy medicine on my lips, and let this kiss
    Repair those violent harms that my two sisters
    Have in thy reverence made.
KENT   Kind and dear princess!
CORDELIA Had you not been their father, these white flakes   30
    Did challenge pity of them. Was this a face
    To be opposed against the warring winds?
    Mine enemy's dog,
    Though he had bit me, should have stood that night
    Against my fire. And wast thou fain, poor father,   35
    To hovel thee with swine and rogues forlorn
    In short and musty straw? Alack, alack,
    'Tis wonder that thy life and wits at once
    Had not concluded all. He wakes. Speak to him.
GENTLEMAN Madam, do you; 'tis fittest.   40
CORDELIA How does my royal lord? How fares your majesty?
LEAR You do me wrong to take me out o'th'grave.
    Thou art a soul in bliss, but I am bound
    Upon a wheel of fire, that mine own tears
    Do scald like molten lead.
CORDELIA   Sir, do you know me?   45
LEAR You are a spirit, I know. Where did you die?
CORDELIA Still, still far wide.
GENTLEMAN He's scarce awake. Let him alone a while.
LEAR Where have I been? Where am I? Fair daylight?
    I am mightily abused. I should ev'n die with pity   50
    To see another thus. I know not what to say.
    I will not swear these are my hands. Let's see:
    I feel this pin prick. Would I were assured
    Of my condition.

Cordelia asks her father for his blessing. He attempts to kneel before her. Although still confused, he is calm and recognises Cordelia, who expresses total forgiveness. As Lear leaves, he again asks Cordelia for forgiveness.

The moment of reconciliation. Finding that Cordelia's tears are real convinces Lear of her sincerity. Cordelia's repeated 'No cause' expresses the unconditional love which she has for her father, and which forgives all injuries.

benediction blessing
fond silly
Fourscore eighty
mainly completely

abuse deceive
great rage frenzy
settling calming

CORDELIA   O look upon me, sir,
            And hold your hand in benediction o'er me.   55
            You must not kneel.
LEAR   Pray do not mock me:
            I am a very foolish, fond old man,
            Fourscore and upward,
            Not an hour more nor less; and to deal plainly,
            I fear I am not in my perfect mind.   60
            Methinks I should know you and know this man;
            Yet I am doubtful: for I am mainly ignorant
            What place this is, and all the skill I have
            Remembers not these garments, nor I know not
            Where I did lodge last night. Do not laugh at me,   65
            For, as I am a man, I think this lady
            To be my child Cordelia.
CORDELIA And so I am: I am.
LEAR Be your tears wet? Yes, faith. I pray, weep not.
            If you have poison for me, I will drink it.   70
            I know you do not love me; for your sisters
            Have, as I do remember, done me wrong.
            You have some cause; they have not.
CORDELIA No cause, no cause.
LEAR Am I in France?
KENT   In your own kingdom, sir.   75
LEAR Do not abuse me.
GENTLEMAN Be comforted, good madam. The great rage
            You see is killed in him. Desire him to go in.
            Trouble him no more till further settling.
CORDELIA Will't please your highness walk?   80
LEAR You must bear with me. Pray you now, forget
            And forgive. I am old and foolish.
                                                Exeunt

Looking back at Act 4
Activities for groups or individuals

1 Setting the scene

Shakespeare did not specify the scene settings used at the head of each scene in this edition of the play. On the Globe stage, there were few props and little or no scenery. The action flowed swiftly and continuously. Since Shakespeare's time, directors and editors have decided the location for each scene. Remind yourself of the scene settings suggested throughout this edition of the play. Think about how appropriate each one seems to you. Where you disagree with the setting chosen, suggest an alternative, giving reasons for your choice.

2 Clothes, costume, disguises and nakedness

There are many moments in Act 4 in which clothes, changes of costume, disguises and nakedness are mentioned or seem important. Make a list of these examples and then talk together about the links between clothes and personal identity.

3 Edmond

Edmond only appears in Scene 2 of Act 4, and speaks just one line, 'Yours in the ranks of death' (Scene 2, line 26). Imagine that Shakespeare thought of giving him a short soliloquy in which he could comment on his progress, on how he views his relationships with Regan and Gonerill, on his feelings about his father, and on his hopes for the future. Write seven or eight lines for Edmond to deliver as an aside after his one line.

4 The road to Dover

By the end of the act, all the major characters are either travelling to Dover or are already there. Establish why each character has chosen to go there, and what they hope to achieve. Speculate about what meetings will take place in Dover during Act 5.

5 The king and the duke

Act 4 has followed the fortunes of two 'old and foolish' men. There are many similarities between their experiences. Summarise what has happened to them during the act. Try to establish similarities and differences in their experience.

Lear and the blinded Gloucester. Find a line from Scene 5 as an appropriate caption for this moment from the Royal Shakespeare Company's 1976 production.

Edmond is unsure if Albany still intends to fight the French invaders.
Regan jealously warns Edmond not to love Gonerill. Albany brings news
that Lear and Cordelia have been joined by British rebels.

1 Regan's jealousy

Regan seems to have forgotten her dead husband, Cornwall. She is pre-occupied by Edmond's relationship with her now-hated sister. She even asks him if he has slept with Gonerill (lines 10–11). What reply would you give to an actor who asks: why does Regan love Edmond so much, and why is she so jealous?

2 What was he about to say?

Edmond's line 14 is interrupted. What do you think he was going to say about Albany and Gonerill? Make up two or three lines for Edmond to say to ease Regan's suspicions.

3 How do they speak: courtesy or contempt? (in groups of three)

Take parts and speak lines 15–26. Each character must decide whether or not to make known their feelings for one another, or whether to hide their emotions under a mask of courtesy. Experiment with different ways of speaking the lines, and decide which version you think is the most dramatically effective.

---

course plans
constant pleasure firm decision
Our sister's … miscarried something's happened to Oswald
forfended forbidden
I never … her I won't have her as a rival
well bemet welcome

With others … out with rebels against the harshness of our rule
Why is this … reasoned why go into that now?
domestic … broils internal arguments
th'ancient … proceeding senior officers about our battle plan

ACT 5 SCENE 1
The British camp near Dover

Enter with drum and colours, EDMOND, REGAN, *Officers and Soldiers*

EDMOND *[To an Officer]* Know of the duke if his last purpose hold,
    Or whether since he is advised by aught
    To change the course. He's full of alteration
    And self-reproving. Bring his constant pleasure.
                                 [Exit Officer]
REGAN Our sister's man is certainly miscarried.   5
EDMOND 'Tis to be doubted, madam.
REGAN   Now, sweet lord,
    You know the goodness I intend upon you.
    Tell me but truly, but then speak the truth,
    Do you not love my sister?
EDMOND   In honoured love.
REGAN But have you never found my brother's way   10
    To the forfended place?
EDMOND   No, by mine honour, madam.
REGAN I never shall endure her. Dear my lord,
    Be not familiar with her.
EDMOND   Fear me not.
    She and the duke her husband –

Enter with drum and colours, ALBANY, GONERILL, *Soldiers*

ALBANY Our very loving sister, well bemet.   15
    Sir, this I heard: the king is come to his daughter,
    With others whom the rigour of our state
    Forced to cry out.
REGAN   Why is this reasoned?
GONERILL Combine together 'gainst the enemy;
    For these domestic and particular broils   20
    Are not the question here.
ALBANY Let's then determine with th'ancient of war
    On our proceeding.
REGAN   Sister, you'll go with us?
GONERILL No.
REGAN 'Tis most convenient. Pray, go with us.   25
GONERILL *[Aside]* O ho, I know the riddle. – I will go.

Gonerill suspects Regan. Edgar gives Albany a letter: a warrior will verify
it if Albany is victorious. Edmond reveals that he has sworn love to both
sisters. He wishes to see Albany, Lear and Cordelia dead.

1 What's the riddle?

Gonerill changes her mind, and leaves with Regan and Albany to discuss the battle plan. Her remark about the riddle (line 26) suggests that
she knows the reason for Regan's invitation. Decide what you think is
running through Gonerill's mind at this moment.

2 Two brothers together? (in pairs)

Some directors ignore the stage direction at line 28 and keep Edmond
on stage for Edgar's words with Albany. What effect on the audience
could a director hope to achieve by having the two brothers together at
this point? List your ideas.

3 Decisions! Decisions! (in groups of six)

In lines 44–58, Edmond reviews his prospects. In rehearsal, actors
sometimes use the following activity to bring out the full implications of
his soliloquy. Take parts as Edmond, Gonerill, Regan, Albany, Lear and
Cordelia. Stand in a circle. Edmond walks around the space speaking
his lines to each of the characters as they are mentioned, adding gestures where they seem appropriate.

---

avouchèd claimed
miscarry lose
machination all plots
diligent discovery careful
  reconnaissance
We will greet the time I can't wait
  to start

carry out my side achieve my aims,
  play my part
countenance power, support
taking off murder
state well-being
defend, not to debate act, not talk

Enter EDGAR [*dressed like a peasant*]

EDGAR If e'er your grace had speech with man so poor,
    Hear me one word.
ALBANY [*To the others*]   I'll overtake you.
                       Exeunt both the armies
    Speak.
EDGAR Before you fight the battle, ope this letter.
    If you have victory, let the trumpet sound   30
    For him that brought it. Wretched though I seem,
    I can produce a champion that will prove
    What is avouchèd there. If you miscarry,
    Your business of the world hath so an end,
    And machination ceases. Fortune love you.   35
ALBANY Stay till I have read the letter.
EDGAR   I was forbid it.
    When time shall serve, let but the herald cry,
    And I'll appear again.   *Exit*
ALBANY Why, fare thee well. I will o'erlook thy paper.

Enter EDMOND

EDMOND The enemy's in view; draw up your powers.   40
    Here is the guess of their true strength and forces
    By diligent discovery; but your haste
    Is now urged on you.
ALBANY   We will greet the time.   *Exit*
EDMOND To both these sisters have I sworn my love,
    Each jealous of the other as the stung   45
    Are of the adder. Which of them shall I take?
    Both? one? or neither? Neither can be enjoyed
    If both remain alive. To take the widow
    Exasperates, makes mad her sister Gonerill,
    And hardly shall I carry out my side,   50
    Her husband being alive. Now then, we'll use
    His countenance for the battle, which being done,
    Let her who would be rid of him devise
    His speedy taking off. As for the mercy
    Which he intends to Lear and to Cordelia,   55
    The battle done, and they within our power,
    Shall never see his pardon; for my state
    Stands on me to defend, not to debate.   *Exit*

Edgar leaves Gloucester, but returns with the news that Albany's forces have won. Edgar comforts Gloucester. Edmond orders the imprisonment of Cordelia and Lear. Cordelia expresses compassion for Lear.

1 Staging the futility of war (in small groups)

The battle at Dover is fought off-stage ('*within*': stage direction, line 4), but many productions choose to show the fighting, or its consequences. For example, in one 1993 production, a line of refugees appeared, some wheeling their belongings in supermarket trolleys, and the hanged body of the Fool was revealed upstage. This was hauntingly reminiscent of the civil war in Bosnia, media coverage of which would have been familiar to a 1993 audience. Work out your own practical ideas for staging the horror of the effects of war.

2 'Ripeness is all' (in pairs)

After the battle, Edgar finds Gloucester wishing for death ('a man may rot'). Edgar tries to lift his father's spirits. Lines 9–11 seem to say that the time of death is chosen by the gods. We should suffer death as we suffer birth, as a natural part of life. Some people find Edgar's words a stoic acceptance of Fate, others find in them a pessimistic resignation to what might, in fact, be changed. What do you think? Talk together about your preferred interpretation.

3 Edmond's entrance 'in conquest' (in large groups)

Set the mood for this ominous final scene by staging the entrance of the triumphant Edmond with his royal prisoners.

---

good host shelter	**meaning** intention
ta'en captured	**incurred** suffered
good guard watch them carefully	**cast down** laid low, humbled
their greater pleasures the wishes of our superiors	**Myself could … outfrown** I could withstand bad luck if it was only me in trouble
censure judge	

ACT 5   SCENE 2
The countryside near Dover

Alarum within. Enter with drum and colours, LEAR, CORDELIA,
and Soldiers, over the stage, and exeunt

Enter EDGAR, dressed like a peasant, and GLOUCESTER

EDGAR Here, father, take the shadow of this tree
  For your good host; pray that the right may thrive.
  If ever I return to you again
  I'll bring you comfort.
GLOUCESTER   Grace go with you, sir.
               Exit [Edgar]

  Alarum and retreat within. Enter EDGAR

EDGAR Away, old man! Give me thy hand; away!   5
  King Lear hath lost, he and his daughter ta'en.
  Give me thy hand. Come on.
GLOUCESTER No further, sir; a man may rot even here.
EDGAR What, in ill thoughts again? Men must endure
  Their going hence even as their coming hither: 10
  Ripeness is all. Come on.
GLOUCESTER   And that's true too.
               Exeunt

ACT 5   SCENE 3
The British camp near Dover

Enter in conquest with drum and colours EDMOND; LEAR and
CORDELIA, as prisoners; Soldiers; CAPTAIN

EDMOND Some officers take them away: good guard,
  Until their greater pleasures first be known
  That are to censure them.
CORDELIA   We are not the first
  Who with best meaning have incurred the worst.
  For thee, oppressèd king, I am cast down,   5
  Myself could else outfrown false fortune's frown.
  Shall we not see these daughters and these sisters?

Lear is joyful to be imprisoned forever with Cordelia. They will mock the petty quarrels of the court. Edmond gives Lear and Cordelia's death warrant to the Captain. He promises promotion and warns against soft-heartedness.

'Come, let's away to prison.' Read lines 8–26 and think about how appropriately you feel this Russian film catches the biblical echoes of the language and the vulnerability of Lear and Cordelia in captivity.

1 The making of a war criminal (in pairs)

Those who commit atrocities in war, whether it be in Nazi Germany in the 1940s or Rwanda in the 1990s, invariably claim that they had no choice but to follow the orders of their superiors. No doubt the Captain would offer the same defence. Take parts and act out lines 27–38, emphasising the control which Edmond has over the Captain. Explore ways of conveying Edmond's sinister authority. Should he speak threateningly or persuasively?

---

gilded butterflies overdressed poseurs
take upon's ... things learn the hidden meanings of the universe
brand flaming torch
shall bring ... foxes will need the gods' help to divide us

goodyears plagues
fell skin
One step ... thee I've already promoted you once
men / Are as the time is morality changes with circumstances
become a sword suit a soldier

LEAR No, no, no, no! Come, let's away to prison.
We two alone will sing like birds i'th'cage.
When thou dost ask me blessing, I'll kneel down   10
And ask of thee forgiveness: so we'll live,
And pray, and sing, and tell old tales, and laugh
At gilded butterflies, and hear poor rogues
Talk of court news, and we'll talk with them too –
Who loses and who wins; who's in, who's out –   15
And take upon 's the mystery of things,
As if we were God's spies; and we'll wear out
In a walled prison packs and sects of great ones
That ebb and flow by th'moon.
EDMOND   Take them away.
LEAR Upon such sacrifices, my Cordelia,   20
The gods themselves throw incense. Have I caught thee?
He that parts us shall bring a brand from heaven
And fire us hence like foxes. Wipe thine eyes.
The goodyears shall devour them, flesh and fell,
Ere they shall make us weep. We'll see 'em starved first.   25
Come.

                    Exeunt Lear and Cordelia, guarded

EDMOND Come hither, captain. Hark.
Take thou this note. Go follow them to prison.
One step I have advanced thee; if thou dost
As this instructs thee, thou dost make thy way   30
To noble fortunes. Know thou this: that men
Are as the time is; to be tender-minded
Does not become a sword. Thy great employment
Will not bear question: either say thou'lt do't,
Or thrive by other means.
CAPTAIN   I'll do't, my lord.   35
EDMOND About it, and write 'happy' when th'hast done.
Mark, I say, instantly, and carry it so
As I have set it down.

                              Exit Captain

Albany demands that Edmond hand over Lear and Cordelia. Edmond delays, provoking Albany to assert Edmond's social inferiority. Regan defends Edmond. Gonerill resents Regan's patronage of Edmond.

1 Enmity becomes explicit

Shakespeare structures his play to great dramatic effect. The tone of this meeting is different from the touching exchange between the captive Lear and Cordelia seen only minutes earlier. Now, the tensions between the victorious allies come to the surface: Edmond and Albany clash, and the sisters bicker.

As a director, identify the points at which you would emphasise the formal courtesy breaking down. Which lines would you want your actors to use as insults?

2 Echoes of the clear-eyed Fool?

Albany's taunt (line 64) that Regan speaks as if Edmond is going to marry her provokes a sharp response from Regan. Her words contain an echo of the Fool, who so clearly predicted the ill effects of Lear giving away his kingdom. Lear's daughters can now see each other's scheming clearly. Gonerill's put-down of her sister, 'That eye that told you so' (line 66), is probably based on the proverb, 'Love, being jealous, makes a good eye look asquint' (jealous people see things wrongly).

Once again, the imagery of distorted perception which runs through the play is employed. It is also hinted at in lines 49–50 ('turn ... eyes': blind ourselves with our own weapons; make our conscripted soldiers rebel). As you read to the end of the play, make a note of references to damaged sight and think about how the theme of moral blindness is important to the whole story.

---

strain nature
Whose age ... it since Lear's old age provokes sympathy
common bosom public sympathy, the hearts of the people
I hold ... brother you're my subordinate not my equal

we list I choose
Bore ... person acted on my behalf
The which immediacy and that connection
compeers equals

Flourish. Enter ALBANY, GONERILL, REGAN, [*Officers,*] *Soldiers*

ALBANY Sir, you have showed today your valiant strain,
         And fortune led you well. You have the captives   40
         Who were the opposites of this day's strife.
         I do require them of you, so to use them
         As we shall find their merits and our safety
         May equally determine.
EDMOND   Sir, I thought it fit
         To send the old and miserable king   45
         To some retention and appointed guard,
         Whose age had charms in it, whose title more,
         To pluck the common bosom on his side
         And turn our impressed lances in our eyes
         Which do command them. With him I sent the queen: 50
         My reason all the same, and they are ready
         Tomorrow, or at further space, t'appear
         Where you shall hold your session.
ALBANY   Sir, by your patience,
         I hold you but a subject of this war,
         Not as a brother.
REGAN   That's as we list to grace him.   55
         Methinks our pleasure might have been demanded
         Ere you had spoke so far. He led our powers,
         Bore the commission of my place and person,
         The which immediacy may well stand up
         And call itself your brother.
GONERILL   Not so hot.   60
         In his own grace he doth exalt himself
         More than in your addition.
REGAN   In my rights,
         By me invested, he compeers the best.
ALBANY That were the most if he should husband you.
REGAN Jesters do oft prove prophets.
GONERILL   Holla, holla!   65
         That eye that told you so, looked but asquint.

Regan betrothes herself to Edmond. Albany forbids the marriage, accusing Edmond and Gonerill of treason and adultery. Albany challenges Edmond to a duel. He accepts. Regan falls ill, poisoned by Gonerill.

1 Regan claims Edmond (in pairs)

Edmond could not decide between the two sisters in Act 5 Scene 1, lines 44–54. Now Regan has chosen for him! Like a city at the end of a siege, she surrenders everything to him ('the walls is thine'). She demands that the whole world witness that Edmond is now her lord and master. How could the actor playing Edmond show his response to this very public proposal? As Regan and Edmond, try different ways of speaking and reacting to lines 68–72.

2 What is Edmond's status? (in small groups)

In lines 54–5, Albany stressed Edmond's social inferiority, treating him as a subject rather than as an equal. Now he further emphasises Edmond's lower social status, calling him 'Half-blooded fellow', and arresting him for treason. Albany also uses the familiar pronoun 'thee', often an insult to someone of noble blood (who would expect to be called 'you'). Yet because Edmond is now Earl of Gloucester, Albany challenges him to personal combat as an aristocratic equal. Suggest how you would stage each stage direction '*Throws down a glove*' to show Albany's contempt and Edmond's response.

3 'Gilded serpent'

Albany's insult (line 78) is directed at Gonerill and probably scorns her lavish clothing. It could carry such meanings as over-dressed, gold plated or guilty. Draw a picture of Gonerill based on a 'gilded serpent'.

From a full-flowing stomach with the full force of anger
patrimony father's inheritance
let-alone permission
Half-blooded semi–noble, bastard
in thy attaint also your dishonourable accomplice
subcontracted already promised
banns public intention to marry
make ... bespoke try your luck with me, as Gonerill is spoken for
An interlude! what a farce!
heinous evil
manifest obvious

REGAN Lady, I am not well, else I should answer
From a full-flowing stomach. [*To Edmond*] General,
Take thou my soldiers, prisoners, patrimony.
Dispose of them, of me; the walls is thine. 70
Witness the world that I create thee here
My lord and master.
GONERILL   Mean you to enjoy him?
ALBANY The let-alone lies not in your good will.
EDMOND Nor in thine, lord.
ALBANY   Half-blooded fellow, yes.
REGAN [*To Edmond*] Let the drum strike, and prove my title thine. 75
ALBANY Stay yet, hear reason. Edmond, I arrest thee
On capital treason, and in thy attaint
This gilded serpent. For your claim, fair sister,
I bar it in the interest of my wife.
'Tis she is subcontracted to this lord, 80
And I, her husband, contradict your banns.
If you will marry, make your love to me,
My lady is bespoke.
GONERILL   An interlude!
ALBANY Thou art armed, Gloucester; let the trumpet sound.
If none appear to prove upon thy person 85
Thy heinous, manifest, and many treasons,
There is my pledge!
          [*Throws down a glove*]
                    I'll make it on thy heart,
Ere I taste bread, thou art in nothing less
Than I have here proclaimed thee.
REGAN   Sick, O sick!
GONERILL [*Aside*] If not, I'll ne'er trust medicine. 90
EDMOND There's my exchange!
          [*Throws down a glove*]
                    What in the world he is
That names me traitor, villain-like he lies.
Call by the trumpet: he that dares, approach;
On him, on you – who not? – I will maintain
My truth and honour firmly.

Albany has dismissed Edmond's soldiers, so Edmond must fight alone. Regan, sick, is taken to Albany's tent. At the third trumpet call, Edgar appears, disguised and armed. Refusing to give his name, he challenges Edmond.

1 The challenge (in small groups)

Shakespeare makes the audience wait for the arrival of Edgar. Formal language and ritual emphasise that the traditional rules of chivalry are at work, governing the encounter of the two knights. At the third trumpet, Edgar finally appears. In some productions, he is dressed in shining armour, like a knight in a medieval tournament. Other productions present him still dressed as a poor man. He and Edmond exchange elaborate words before they fight.

a Take parts and work out how to stage lines 100–40. Suggest how to heighten the drama in the delayed entrance of Edgar, and how to deliver the formal, but often hate-filled, language which the characters speak before the duel.

b A psychoanalyst might attribute Edgar's changing disguises to an identity crisis brought on by the trauma of his brother's treachery. This could explain his refusal to give his name. Do you find this explanation convincing? Give reasons for your agreement or disagreement with the 'identity crisis' theory.

c Edgar uses a vivid image of biting and devouring when he claims 'my name is lost, by treason's tooth bare-gnawn and canker-bit' (worm-eaten). Imagine that you have been invited to design a costume for Edgar based on this imagery. Sketch your ideas.

---

thy single virtue your one good quality (your bravery)
levied recruited
Took their discharge been dismissed

quality or degree nobility and rank
lists list of officers
manifold prolific
adversary opponent
cope fight

ALBANY   A herald, ho!   95

Enter a HERALD

Trust to thy single virtue, for thy soldiers,
All levied in my name, have in my name
Took their discharge.
REGAN   My sickness grows upon me.
ALBANY She is not well. Convey her to my tent.
                              [Exit Regan, led by an Officer]
Come hither, herald. Let the trumpet sound,   100
And read out this.
                    A trumpet sounds
HERALD *Reads* 'If any man of quality or degree within the lists of
    the army will maintain upon Edmond, supposed Earl of
    Gloucester, that he is a manifold traitor, let him appear by the
    third sound of the trumpet. He is bold in his defence.'   105
                    First trumpet
Again.
                    Second trumpet
Again.
                    Third trumpet

Trumpet answers within. Enter EDGAR, *armed*

ALBANY Ask him his purposes, why he appears
        Upon this call o'th'trumpet.
HERALD   What are you?
        Your name, your quality, and why you answer   110
        This present summons?
EDGAR   Know, my name is lost,
        By treason's tooth bare-gnawn and canker-bit.
        Yet am I noble as the adversary
        I come to cope.
ALBANY   Which is that adversary?
EDGAR What's he that speaks for Edmond, Earl of Gloucester?   115
EDMOND Himself. What sayst thou to him?

*Edgar proclaims Edmond's treachery. Edmond denies his guilt. Edmond is
fatally wounded in the fight. Albany shows Gonerill's letter to Edmond.
Gonerill attempts to seize it, claiming to be ruler and law-maker.*

Identify each character, and suggest which line you think is being spoken
at this precise moment.

Maugre in spite of
fire-new fortune recent honour (as
  duke)
bent determined
say of breeding proof of nobility
safe and nicely legally and
  according to the rules

give them instant way despatch
  them
practice cheating
cozened and beguiled tricked and
  deceived
arraign prosecute

EDGAR   Draw thy sword,
        That if my speech offend a noble heart
        Thy arm may do thee justice. Here is mine.
        Behold, it is the privilege of mine honour,
        My oath, and my profession. I protest,   120
        Maugre thy strength, place, youth, and eminence,
        Despite thy victor-sword and fire-new fortune,
        Thy valour and thy heart, thou art a traitor:
        False to thy gods, thy brother, and thy father,
        Conspirant 'gainst this high illustrious prince,   125
        And from th'extremest upward of thy head
        To the descent and dust below thy foot,
        A most toad-spotted traitor. Say thou no,
        This sword, this arm, and my best spirits are bent
        To prove upon thy heart, whereto I speak,   130
        Thou liest.
EDMOND   In wisdom I should ask thy name,
        But since thy outside looks so fair and warlike,
        And that thy tongue some say of breeding breathes,
        What safe and nicely I might well delay
        By rule of knighthood, I disdain and spurn.   135
        Back do I toss these treasons to thy head,
        With the hell-hated lie o'erwhelm thy heart,
        Which, for they yet glance by and scarcely bruise,
        This sword of mine shall give them instant way
        Where they shall rest for ever. Trumpets, speak!   140
                Alarums. [They] fight. [Edmond falls]
ALBANY Save him, save him.
GONERILL   This is practice, Gloucester;
        By th'law of war thou wast not bound to answer
        An unknown opposite. Thou art not vanquished,
        But cozened and beguiled.
ALBANY   Shut your mouth, dame,
        Or with this paper shall I stop it. – Hold, sir.   145
        Thou worse than any name, read thine own evil. –
        No tearing, lady. I perceive you know it.
GONERILL Say if I do; the laws are mine, not thine.
        Who can arraign me for't?   *Exit*
ALBANY   Most monstrous! O,
        Know'st thou this paper?

An officer is sent to watch over Gonerill. The dying Edmond confesses his crimes. Edgar sheds his disguise and tells how, as Poor Tom, he helped Gloucester, only revealing his identity to his father afterwards.

1 Reconciled in death? (in pairs)

Edmond forgives his killer and Edgar exchanges 'charity' before revealing his identity. Edgar affirms that 'the gods are just' for punishing both Edmond and Gloucester for their sins of pleasure. Edmond acknowledges the role of providence in his demise, returning him 'full circle' to the bottom of the wheel of fortune. At this point, the two actors must decide how sincerely Edmond and Edgar are reconciled with one another. Make up your own mind by trying the following activity.

Take parts and speak lines 152–64. First, emphasise genuine reconciliation. Then stress insincerity on the part of one or both brothers. Decide what gesture Edmond could use to accompany 'I am here' (line 164).

2 Edgar's story (in groups of four or five)

a Edgar recapitulates the 'brief tale' of his life as Poor Tom. As one person speaks lines 174–90, the others show a mimed version of Edgar's summary of his life since his betrayal by Edmond.

b Edgar describes how he saved Gloucester 'from despair', yet blames himself for not shedding his disguise sooner ('O fault!', line 183). Suggest why Edgar reproaches himself so bitterly, even though he comforted his father so tenderly in his last hours.

---

govern look after
thou / That hast ... on who has better luck than
blood nobility
of our pleasant vices ... us turn our pleasure-giving sins into pains

The dark ... got his sordid fathering of you
That we the pain ... once! suffering is preferable to death
habit disguise
rings eyes

EDMOND   Ask me not what I know.   150
ALBANY Go after her, she's desperate, govern her.
                                    [*Exit an Officer*]
EDMOND What you have charged me with, that have I done,
    And more, much more; the time will bring it out.
    'Tis past, and so am I. But what art thou
    That hast this fortune on me? If thou'rt noble,   155
    I do forgive thee.
EDGAR   Let's exchange charity.
    I am no less in blood than thou art, Edmond.
    If more, the more th'hast wronged me.
    My name is Edgar, and thy father's son.
    The gods are just, and of our pleasant vices   160
    Make instruments to plague us.
    The dark and vicious place where thee he got
    Cost him his eyes.
EDMOND   Th'hast spoken right; 'tis true.
    The wheel is come full circle; I am here.
ALBANY Methought thy very gait did prophesy   165
    A royal nobleness. I must embrace thee.
    Let sorrow split my heart if ever I
    Did hate thee or thy father.
EDGAR Worthy prince, I know't.
ALBANY Where have you hid yourself?   170
    How have you known the miseries of your father?
EDGAR By nursing them, my lord. List a brief tale,
    And when 'tis told, O that my heart would burst!
    The bloody proclamation to escape
    That followed me so near (O, our lives' sweetness,   175
    That we the pain of death would hourly die
    Rather than die at once!) taught me to shift
    Into a madman's rags, t'assume a semblance
    That very dogs disdained; and in this habit
    Met I my father with his bleeding rings,   180
    Their precious stones new-lost; became his guide,
    Led him, begged for him, saved him from despair,
    Never – O fault! – revealed myself unto him
    Until some half hour past, when I was armed.

Edgar reports that Gloucester died happily, News comes of Gonerill's suicide and Regan's poisoning. Kent arrives to bid farewell to Lear. Albany demands that Edmond reveal the whereabouts of Lear and Cordelia.

1 A joke in the face of death

Both Gonerill and Regan die off-stage. Edmond greets the news with what could be a grim joke against his own agreement to marry both of them (lines 202–3). If you were playing Edmond, decide if you would want to make the audience smile at this point. Would humour add to or detract from the horror of this death-ridden scene?

2 'Produce the bodies'

Albany orders the bodies of the dead sisters to be carried on. He echoes Edgar and Edmond's lines 160–4 in affirming the all powerful 'judgement of the heavens'. Decide how you would stage the bringing-in of the bodies: casually, with great ceremony, or in some other manner? Also suggest how Albany should react to seeing his dead wife.

3 Kent's freedom

The loyal Kent appears *'as himself'* to bid farewell to Lear, perhaps for the last time. Although he fought on Lear's side, Kent has freedom of movement, and does not seem to be a prisoner. Suggest how you could ensure that the audience realises that Kent has dropped his disguise as Caius and is now appearing as his true self.

of this good success victory in the duel
our pilgrimage about our journey together
flawed weakened
smilingly and he died happily

perchance perhaps
contracted engaged
marry unite
the compliment ... urges the greeting that courtesy would normally demand

Not sure, though hoping of this good success,   185
I asked his blessing, and from first to last
Told him our pilgrimage; but his flawed heart –
Alack, too weak the conflict to support –
'Twixt two extremes of passion, joy and grief,
Burst smilingly.
EDMOND   This speech of yours hath moved me,   190
And shall perchance do good. But speak you on,
You look as you had something more to say.
ALBANY If there be more, more woeful, hold it in,
For I am almost ready to dissolve,
Hearing of this.   195

Enter a GENTLEMAN [*with a bloody knife*]

GENTLEMAN Help, help, O help!
EDGAR   What kind of help?
ALBANY   Speak, man.
EDGAR What means this bloody knife?
GENTLEMAN   'Tis hot, it smokes.
It came even from the heart of – O, she's dead.
ALBANY Who dead? Speak, man.
GENTLEMAN Your lady, sir, your lady; and her sister   200
By her is poisoned: she confesses it.
EDMOND I was contracted to them both; all three
Now marry in an instant.
EDGAR   Here comes Kent.

Enter KENT [*as himself*]

ALBANY Produce the bodies, be they alive or dead.
Gonerill's and Regan's bodies brought out
This judgement of the heavens, that makes us tremble,   205
Touches us not with pity. – O, is this he?
[*To Kent*] The time will not allow the compliment
Which very manners urges.
KENT   I am come
To bid my king and master aye good night.
Is he not here?
ALBANY   Great thing of us forgot!   210
Speak, Edmond; where's the king, and where's Cordelia?
Seest thou this object, Kent?

Edmond urges that someone be sent to cancel his death warrant on Lear and Cordelia. She was to be hanged to give the appearance of suicide. Lear enters, carrying the dead Cordelia and grieving for her.

'Howl, howl, howl, howl!' The entrance of Lear carrying the dead Cordelia is one of the most famous and heart-rending scenes in world drama. Here, moments later, Lear searches Cordelia's face for signs of life. The sight prompts Kent to ask if the end of the world has come (line 237). In the seventeenth century, to satisfy audience demand for a happy ending, Nahum Tate rewrote Act 5 so that Cordelia survives (see page 228).

writ death warrant
office task (of killing Lear and Cordelia)
commission orders

fordid killed
the promised end the end of the world, Judgement Day

KENT   Alack, why thus?
EDMOND Yet Edmond was beloved.
          The one the other poisoned for my sake,
          And after slew herself.   215
ALBANY Even so. – Cover their faces.
EDMOND I pant for life. Some good I mean to do,
          Despite of mine own nature. Quickly send –
          Be brief in it – to th'castle; for my writ
          Is on the life of Lear and on Cordelia.   220
          Nay, send in time.
ALBANY   Run, run, O run!
EDGAR To who, my lord? – Who has the office? Send
          Thy token of reprieve.
EDMOND Well thought on. Take my sword. The captain,
          Give it the captain.
EDGAR   Haste thee for thy life.   225
                              [*Exit an Officer*]
EDMOND He hath commission from thy wife and me
          To hang Cordelia in the prison and
          To lay the blame upon her own despair,
          That she fordid herself.
ALBANY The gods defend her. Bear him hence a while.   230
                              [*Edmond is borne off*]

Enter LEAR *with* CORDELIA *in his arms* [*and the* OFFICER *following*]

LEAR Howl, howl, howl, howl! O, you are men of stones.
          Had I your tongues and eyes, I'd use them so,
          That heaven's vault should crack. She's gone for ever.
          I know when one is dead and when one lives.
          She's dead as earth.
                      [*He lays her down*]
                              Lend me a looking-glass;   235
          If that her breath will mist or stain the stone,
          Why then she lives.
KENT   Is this the promised end?
EDGAR Or image of that horror?
ALBANY   Fall and cease.

Lear desperately seeks for signs that Cordelia lives. He boasts that he killed her murderer. Filled with grief, he is unmoved by the reunion with Kent or by the deaths of his other daughters. Edmond is reported dead.

Lear grieves for Cordelia. Choose one of Lear's lines as a caption.

redeem cure
falchion curved sword
crosses troubles
spoil disable
brag boast
That from ... steps I've followed your decline from the very start

Nor no man else no one's welcome here, if not me
fordone killed
present us to bother, question, talk with
bootless futile

LEAR This feather stirs, she lives: if it be so,
    It is a chance which does redeem all sorrows 240
    That ever I have felt.
KENT   O my good master!
LEAR Prithee, away.
EDGAR   'Tis noble Kent, your friend.
LEAR A plague upon you murderers, traitors all.
    I might have saved her; now she's gone for ever.
    Cordelia, Cordelia, stay a little. Ha? 245
    What is't thou sayst? – Her voice was ever soft,
    Gentle, and low, an excellent thing in woman. –
    I killed the slave that was a-hanging thee.
OFFICER 'Tis true, my lords, he did.
LEAR   Did I not, fellow?
    I have seen the day with my good biting falchion 250
    I would have made them skip. I am old now,
    And these same crosses spoil me. [*To Kent*] Who are you?
    Mine eyes are not o'th'best, I'll tell you straight.
KENT If fortune brag of two she loved and hated,
    One of them we behold. 255
LEAR This' a dull sight. Are you not Kent?
KENT   The same,
    Your servant Kent. Where is your servant Caius?
LEAR He's a good fellow, I can tell you that.
    He'll strike, and quickly too. He's dead and rotten.
KENT No, my good lord, I am the very man – 260
LEAR I'll see that straight.
KENT That from your first of difference and decay
    Have followed your sad steps.
LEAR   You're welcome hither.
KENT Nor no man else. All's cheerless, dark, and deadly.
    Your eldest daughters have fordone themselves 265
    And desperately are dead.
LEAR   Ay, so I think.
ALBANY He knows not what he says, and vain is it
    That we present us to him.

Enter a MESSENGER

EDGAR   Very bootless.
MESSENGER Edmond is dead, my lord.

Albany returns authority to Lear. Lear again grieves for Cordelia, then dies.
Albany asks Edgar and Kent to share power. Kent hints that he has not long
to live. Edgar urges plain speaking, not dishonest formality.

1 Lear's last lines (in pairs)

How would you advise the actor playing Lear to deliver his final lines
279–85? Try acting out different interpretations before you decide.

a 'Never, never, never, never, never.' Experiment with possible ways of
speaking line 282. Also consider other repetitions in Lear's final lines,
and suggest how they add to the poignancy of the speech.

b 'And my poor fool is hanged.' In Shakespeare's time, 'fool' was often
used as a term of affection. Do you think Lear is referring to Cordelia
or to the Fool here?

c 'Look there, look there.' What does Lear see? Lear's dying words are
often spoken as he searches Cordelia's face for signs of life. But in one
production, Lear seemed to die joyously as he glimpsed something
hopeful and beautiful in the far distance. As one critic wrote, 'Who
knows what Lear has seen as he pulls himself and Cordelia into another
world?'. How would you want to see Lear's final line performed?

2 Final words

In the quarto version of the play (see page 232), Shakespeare gave lines
297–300 to Albany. Decide, with reasons, who you think should have the
last word: Edgar, Albany, or one of the other survivors.

3 'Exeunt with a dead march'

What would be the final image the audience would see in your production of the play?

---

trifle triviality
What comfort ... applied
everything will be done to help the
nation and King Lear
boot, and such addition extra
titles
wages reward

rack instrument of torture (used to
stretch the victim's limbs)
usurped stole
Bear them carry the bodies
twain two
the gored state sustain care for
this damaged nation

ALBANY   That's but a trifle here.
        You lords and noble friends, know our intent.   270
        What comfort to this great decay may come
        Shall be applied. For us, we will resign
        During the life of this old majesty
        To him our absolute power; [*To Edgar and Kent*] you, to
                your rights,
        With boot, and such addition as your honours   275
        Have more than merited. All friends shall taste
        The wages of their virtue, and all foes
        The cup of their deservings. O see, see!
LEAR And my poor fool is hanged. No, no, no life?
        Why should a dog, a horse, a rat have life,   280
        And thou no breath at all? Thou'lt come no more,
        Never, never, never, never, never.
        Pray you, undo this button. Thank you, sir.
        Do you see this? Look on her! Look, her lips.
        Look there, look there.   *He dies*
EDGAR   He faints. My lord, my lord!   285
KENT Break, heart, I prithee break.
EDGAR   Look up, my lord.
KENT Vex not his ghost. O, let him pass. He hates him
        That would upon the rack of this tough world
        Stretch him out longer.
EDGAR   He is gone indeed.
KENT The wonder is he hath endured so long.   290
        He but usurped his life.
ALBANY Bear them from hence. Our present business
        Is general woe. Friends of my soul, you twain
        Rule in this realm and the gored state sustain.
KENT I have a journey, sir, shortly to go: 295
        My master calls me; I must not say no.
EDGAR The weight of this sad time we must obey,
        Speak what we feel, not what we ought to say.
        The oldest hath borne most; we that are young
        Shall never see so much, nor live so long.   300
                        Exeunt with a dead march

Looking back at the play
Activities for groups or individuals

---

1 Enjoying tragedy?

In spite of all its cruelty and bleakness, *King Lear* is one of Shakespeare's most popular plays, frequently performed. Talk together about what audiences can gain from seeing the play. Do you think it is possible to enjoy *King Lear*?

2 Mourning Cordelia

This activity can help you to share the intensity of Lear's words at the death of Cordelia. You could try it in the hall or the drama studio, but it can be just as effective in a classroom, especially if it 'blacks out'. Everyone in the class can be involved.

a Identify all the phrases or sentences in Act 5 Scene 3, lines 230–69 which express grief or sympathy for Cordelia or Lear. Write them on pieces of paper, and distribute them to everyone except Cordelia. Each person memorises their phrase or sentence of mourning language.

b Make a tableau of Lear and the dead Cordelia surrounded by a circle of sympathetic onlookers.

c Make the tableau again. This time, speak your memorised words in turn as a soundtrack to the picture. Use stage lights or candles and, at low volume, play appropriate music to add atmosphere.

d Try introducing movement. For example, each mourner could, in turn, step into the circle, then move close to Lear and Cordelia, adding gesture to emphasise their words, before returning to the circle of mourning.

3 Unheard voices – the nameless characters

Throughout the play, minor, unnamed characters appear and speak: a captain, an old man, a gentleman and some servants. Other nameless characters appear, but do not speak, for example knights, soldiers and attendants. Give one of these 'ordinary' people a voice. Invent a role for yourself as a low-status character in Lear's Britain. Recount what you know of the life and death of King Lear. Your story may be fragmentary, a mixture of briefly glimpsed events, overheard conversations and gossip.

4 'Drum and colours'

The opening stage direction for Act 5 Scene 1 suggests that the scene begins with flags flying and drums beating. Design flags or coats of arms for the soldiers led by Edmond and Regan. You could also do the same for the forces of Albany or Cordelia. Choose symbols for your designs which are appropriate to each character's nature and values.

5 Changing fortunes

The wheel of fortune is an image which recurs throughout *King Lear*. In the course of the play, almost every character experiences a change in their fortunes. Draw a wheel of fortune and place the major characters on it, showing their progress around the wheel as their fortunes change.

6 Most ... to least

Make several lists of the names of all the characters in the play so that they range from 'most' to 'least' along a number of scales. Remember that there is often no one right answer, although some answers can be more firmly justified from the script than others. Analyse your lists to find out what connections you feel exist between them. Here are some example 'scales', but you could also invent your own:

> youngest → oldest
> most likeable → least likeable
> most moral (good) → least moral (bad)
> most reliable → least reliable

7 Time scale

Draw a time line plotting the sequence of events in the play. You could choose to draw your sequence in the style of something like the Bayeux Tapestry.

8 The most interesting question

What is the question you would most like to ask of each of the following: Lear, Cordelia, Edmond, Edgar, the Fool? Write a separate question for each. Then pool all your questions in the class. Decide which are the most interesting, and use them to 'hot seat' members of the class in role as the characters.

9 Modern relevance

Make a list of all the things you would say in a debate about *King Lear*'s relevance to today's world.

Shakespeare finds his story

Why did Shakespeare choose to write a play with a story-line similar to *Cinderella*: a fairy tale about a foolish father, a pair of ugly sisters and one loving, but mistreated daughter? No one can be certain about exactly what led Shakespeare to select this plot, but the following four possibilities may help explain his interest in this particular story in 1605, when he probably wrote the play.

1 The gossip of the day: a topical play?

Real-life stories of old men dividing their wealth between their children and living to regret it provided fascinating material for gossip in the early seventeenth century. Public interest in these lurid tales of greed and suffering amongst the monied classes made them sensational and popular sources of gossip.

During Shakespeare's early years in London, he probably shared the interest Londoners took in the story of Sir William Allen, a former Lord Mayor of the city. Sir William made the mistake, in his old age, of splitting his estate between his three daughters and arranging to live alternately with them. This proved disastrous. Having acquired his wealth, the three women treated their aged father with disrespect, and resented the expense of looking after him. In winter, they even denied him fuel to keep warm. Sir William endured one particular misery from which King Lear was spared; he had no Cordelia, and was mistreated by all three of his daughters.

Sir Brian Annesley, another popular subject of gossip in 1603–4, at least had one child who defended him. She was Cordell, the youngest of his three daughters. In 1603, Sir Brian's eldest daughter tried to have her elderly father certified as a lunatic so that she and her husband could take control of the old man's property and wealth. Her husband wrote that Sir Brian had 'fallen into such imperfection and intemperature of mind and memory as we thought him thereby become altogether unfit to govern himself or his estate'. Cordell challenged her sister in court, protesting that it was unjust to her father 'at his last gasp to be registered a lunatic'. The Annesley case has striking parallels with the *King Lear* story, including the similarity between the names of the sympathetic youngest daughters.

2 The hazards of transferring power: a political play?

The difficulties caused by a royal succession and the perils of a divided kingdom were topics of heated political debate among Shakespeare's audience. *King Lear* is a play in tune with the political issues and anxieties of its time. When Shakespeare wrote it, a new king, James I, had been on the throne of England for only two years.

In seventeenth-century England, inheritance was determined by the tradition of male primogeniture, a system in which the first-born son inherits all his father's wealth and titles. Lack of sons was very dangerous. King Henry VIII had been desperate to have a male heir, but despite six different wives, he was outlived by only one legitimate son, who survived to reign for just six years. By the time *King Lear* was written, England had been ruled by two queens, Mary and Elizabeth. As the unmarried Queen Elizabeth's life drew to a close, there was no male heir. The question of her successor was anxiously discussed, and the threat of civil war was feared.

The folly of dividing a kingdom would have been obvious to Shakespeare's audience. They would certainly understand Kent's sense of outrage at Lear carving up his realm. The official ideology of Shakespeare's time interpreted English history as a steady movement towards the security, strength and cohesion of a single realm. The audiences at the first performances of *King Lear* were all too aware of the recent peaceful succession of King James, who had united the crowns of England and Scotland. The sharp contrast with Lear's actions would have been clear.

3 Legendary stories: a history play?

The first known telling of the story of King Lear and his three daughters is in Geoffrey of Monmouth's *History of England*, written over four hundred years before Shakespeare's day. It was a mixture of myth and legend, but many people in the seventeenth century regarded it as historical fact. A retelling of the legend with which Shakespeare was probably familiar appeared in Raphael Holinshed's *Chronicles of England, Scotlande and Irelande* (1577). Shakespeare had certainly used Holinshed as a source for other plays, and he found there an account of the King Lear story. In summary, it reads as follows:

> Leir, the ageing king of Britain has three daughters, Gonorilla, Regan and Cordeilla, of whom his favourite is the youngest, Cordeilla. In order to help him to decide on the succession, he asks which of his daughters loves him best. Gonorilla and Regan speak extravagantly of the love they bear

their father, but Cordeilla says that she loves him only according to his worth. Leir is furious and arranges for the two older daughters to marry the Dukes of Cornwall and Albany, between whom the kingdom will be divided after his death. The dukes are immediately given half of this inheritance. Cordeilla is to receive nothing, but the Prince of Gallia, who rules a part of France, chooses to marry her despite the fact that she has no dowry.

Cornwall and Albany resent having to wait for power. They rise against Leir, forcing him to give up all his power. Leir's oldest daughters, with whom he has no choice but to live alternately, treat him unkindly and reduce the number of his servants.

Leir flees the kingdom, and travels to Gallia. Before he appears at court, Cordeilla supplies her father with money so that he is able to arrive with clothes and servants befitting a king. Cordeilla and her husband make him welcome.

The Prince of Gallia raises an army to restore Leir to his throne. Cordeilla accompanies her father when he returns to his kingdom, and is named as his heir. The army of the Dukes of Cornwall and Albany is defeated, and the two Dukes die in battle. Leir regains his throne and reigns for two years before he dies. Cordeilla succeeds him, but her reign is cut short by a rebellion led by her sisters' sons. She is imprisoned, despairs and commits suicide. Her nephews then make war against each other, and England is only restored to peace after one of them is killed and the other is able to rule uncontested.

Shakespeare made many alterations and additions to Holinshed's story. He added the characters of the Fool, Kent and Oswald; he invented Lear's madness and the storm; and he inserted the entire sub-plot of Gloucester and his sons. Shakespeare intensified the cruelty and suffering in his play. He has Cordelia die before her father, and so heightens his grief. The play ends with the deaths of Lear's entire family. Although Holinshed tells of Cordelia's suicide, his story sees virtue rewarded and the rightful king restored. There is no such benign ending in *King Lear*.

4 Shakespeare's reading: a literary play?

Shakespeare may have read or seen *The True Chronicle History of King Leir*, a play first performed in the 1590s, but not published until 1605. In this dramatised version of the story, no characters die and Leir is restored to his realm at the end. It contains stage directions of 'thunder and lightning', which may have been Shakespeare's inspiration for the storm in Act 3.

Shakespeare certainly read Samuel Harsnett's *A Declaration of Egregious Popish Impostures*, published in 1603. Much of the strange language used by Edgar when pretending to be the mad Poor Tom, especially the lists of demons' names (see page 138), is taken from this anti-Catholic pamphlet. It claimed to expose the evils of false exorcism (driving out devils from mad people), and quoted speeches supposedly made by people who pretended to be possessed by demons. By giving such evil language to Edgar, a 'good' character, Shakespeare increases the dramatic intensity of the play.

The most significant addition which Shakespeare made to the old legend was the story of Gloucester and his sons. This sub-plot mirrors the main plot of Lear and his daughters. It was based on an episode taken from *Arcadia*, a prose romance story by Sir Philip Sidney, which was first published in 1590. Shakespeare follows the story quite closely, although Sidney's main character is a king rather than an earl. In *Arcadia*, the illegitimate son is directly responsible for blinding his own father after seizing his throne. The virtuous son is betrayed by his brother, loses his father's favour, and is driven into exile. He returns to protect his father, but, while leading the blinded man, he refuses to help him commit suicide. The blind king eventually crowns his virtuous son and dies happy.

The Gloucester sub-plot which Shakespeare added has many similarities with the central story of *King Lear*. Both are about powerful men and their relationships with their grown-up children. Both involve the father's unjust rejection of a faithful child who continues to love and protect the father. Both show the fathers mistreated by the children whom they favour.

In *King Lear*, the sub-plot deepens the atmosphere of horror. The tragic effect of the play is heightened as the sufferings of the two families unfold.

5 A story for today

Imagine that you have been asked to write a modern retelling of the King Lear story. What situation would you use as a modern parallel to the division of the kingdom? You could use the handing over of control and power within a company, a school or a college, the inheritance of land and money, or the division of a dictator's power. Make a list of other possibilities. Consider the advantages and disadvantages of each as a means of telling a similar story. Suggest alternative sub-plots which you could use to intensify the dramatic effect of your main story.

Different views of 'Nature'

The words 'Nature', 'natural' and 'unnatural' occur over forty times in the play. Almost every character appeals in some way to 'nature': either to justify their actions or to help them, or to explain why things are as they are. Lear begins the 'love test' by inviting his daughters to compete for the largest share of his kingdom by combining their natural affection for their father with exaggerated statements of their love ('where nature doth with merit challenge'). But within minutes he rejects Cordelia as 'a wretch whom nature is ashamed / Almost t'acknowledge hers'. Later, he will call Gonerill and Regan 'unnatural hags'.

Why is 'nature' so important in the play? One major reason is that it is a powerful means of controlling people. Like all tyrants, Lear knows that, if he can make everyone believe that it is 'natural' for him to rule and for his every wish to be obeyed, then he has power over them. They will think that what is 'natural' is right, and that it must not be challenged. If daughters think that it is natural to obey all their father's commands, or if people believe that society is naturally hierarchical, with a king at the top, then they are unlikely to challenge that 'natural' state of affairs.

For much of the play, Lear believes that everything he does is natural. Any person who frustrates his desires is unnatural, because it is natural that everyone should obey him without question. His view of his family is the same as his view of England: rigidly hierarchical with himself as father-king at the top, entitled to immediate and unstinting obedience. Nature herself is a goddess to whom he can appeal for revenge on his unnatural daughter ('Hear, Nature, hear…').

One way of understanding the play is to see it as the slow and agonizing transformation of Lear's view of the natural order of things. Through his suffering, Lear's original view of nature is painfully stripped away.

Two views of nature

A traditional way of understanding the play has been to see it as depicting two different views of nature, malign or benign (bad or good). Characters are grouped according to their view of nature. That view defines their opinion of society, of what men and women are like, and of how they should behave. Although this two-fold view of nature is a simple stereotype, it can be a valuable first step in developing your thinking about the significance of 'nature' in the play.

Nature as malign The view of nature as spitefully malevolent links together the ruthless individualism of Edmond, Gonerill and Regan. Nature is seen as a malign force which acts as a powerful motivator. It drives and feeds ruthless and selfish impulses. Humans behave like violent predatory animals, preying on the naïve, innocent and vulnerable. They lack conscience and moral sensitivity, and are concerned only with their own advancement and profit. Like Lear, Edmond thinks of nature as a deity ('Thou, Nature, art my goddess'), but sees her favouring the merciless, self-motivated individual. This 'natural' (illegitimate) son of Gloucester is coldly calculating and cunning. He mocks Gloucester's superstitions, and is scornful of any notion that his nature was determined by the stars.

Gonerill and Regan flatter Lear shamelessly to gain a share of their father's wealth, but then renounce all family bonds and duties. Hard-heartedly, they cruelly exile Lear into the storm.

Nature as benign Gloucester, Kent, Edgar and Cordelia are shaped by a benign vision of nature as a kind-hearted and benevolent force which strives for order, stability and harmony. Gloucester sees the world as orderly and hierarchical, valuing trust, loyalty and family bonds. His response to Edgar's apparent villainy is to proclaim him an 'unnatural, detested, brutish villain'. Kent's loyalty to his master, Lear, expresses itself in his unwavering and unquestioning sympathy and concern for the king throughout the play. Cordelia's nature, like Kent's, is truthful and honest. Her constancy and devotion to Lear act as healing, cleansing forces. Edgar cloaks his true nature in the disguise of a mad beggar, but redeems, heals and restores his father, to whom he remains faithful.

a To help you make up your mind about the appropriateness of the two views of nature given above, work through the list of characters on page 1. Consider each character in turn, and think about to what extent their view of nature is malign or benign.

b Organise a class debate on the following claim: '*King Lear* shows that nothing to do with human society is "natural". Everything is shaped by men and women (mostly men!), and could be otherwise. Nature itself is completely indifferent to human beings.'

Justice in *King Lear*

At the end of the play, Albany confronts the bloody reality of the death and suffering caused by Lear's division of his kingdom. Albany declares that everyone will get precisely what they deserve: 'All friends shall taste/ The wages of their virtue, and all foes / The cup of their deservings'. But do they? Edmond has been killed by the brother he wronged, and the wicked Gonerill and Regan are dead. It is, however, all too evident that justice has not been done. The innocent Cordelia has died cruelly, hanged in prison. Gloucester's blinding and mental suffering hardly fit his 'crime' of fathering the bastard Edmond. Does Lear, for all his flaws of character or judgement, deserve the agonies of madness he has undergone ('I am bound upon a wheel of fire'), or the twisted irony of being reconciled with Cordelia only to have her ruthlessly snatched away from him? If poetic justice means that people get what they deserve, then it seems hard to find it in *King Lear*. What kinds of justice are there in the play?

Divine justice

A belief in the power of divine justice runs through the play. Lear strengthens his early displays of authority and paternal cursing by appeals to pagan deities. He swears by 'the sacred radiance of the sun', 'The mysteries of Hecate and the night', 'the operation of the orbs', 'Apollo' and 'Jupiter'. Albany, seeking an explanation for Lear's cursing of Gonerill, addresses the 'gods that we adore'. Regan appeals to the 'blessed gods' when Lear turns his anger on her. Lear himself begs for help from the 'heavens': 'If you do love old men … send down and take my part', and acknowledges the authority of 'high-judging Jove'.

Attitudes towards the gods see-saw in the play. Sometimes they are seen as 'kind' and 'mighty', at other times arbitrary, indifferent and cruel. Albany finds them just: 'You are above / You justicers'. Gloucester thinks them spitefully unjust: 'As flies to wanton boys are we to th'gods; / They kill us for their sport', then revises his opinion: 'You ever gentle gods'. To Cordelia the gods are benevolent: 'O you kind gods'. Having mortally wounded his brother, Edgar acknowledges that human affairs are watched over, considered and shaped by a divine justice: 'The gods are just, and of our pleasant vices / Make instruments to plague us'.

Human justice

There are five 'trials' in the play in which one human being judges another:

1 Lear's 'love trial' of his three daughters (Act 1 Scene 1). Lear, as judge and jury, metes out the 'justice' he thinks is appropriate.

2 Cornwall's 'trial' of Kent, whose bluntness earns him instant punishment in the stocks (Act 2 Scene 2).

3 Cornwall and Regan's 'trial' of Gloucester (Act 3 Scene 7).

4 Lear's 'mock trial' of Gonerill and Regan. This appears only in the quarto version of the play (see page 233).

5 The trial by battle (Act 5 Scene 3). Edgar challenges Edmond to trial by combat on the charge of treason.

Throughout the play men or women pass judgement on their fellows, always appealing to some higher power or authority. Lear exiles Kent for daring to criticise him; Gloucester impulsively condemns Edgar; Gonerill and Regan, having assumed their father's power, 'judge' Lear and pronounce punishment; Edmond sentences Lear and Cordelia to imprisonment and issues their death warrant.

The play clearly shows that, when humans exercise justice, there is no guarantee that it will be fair, proper or right. Possession of power is more important than fairness. Gonerill sees herself as the queen, unchallengeable, controlling the law and yet beyond it: 'the laws are mine, not thine / Who can arraign me for't?' In his madness, Lear displays piercing insight into the fallibility of judges, and into the way powerful, rich people can avoid punishment for their crimes: 'Plate sin with gold / And the strong lance of justice hurtless breaks'.

But there are incidents in the play which suggest that some kind of natural justice is at work: a servant protests about Gloucester's horrific treatment and slays Cornwall; Gloucester's loyal servant helps his blinded master; and Oswald's attempt to kill a blind old man results in his own death.

Turn to the list of characters on page 1. Consider each character in turn, asking yourself the question 'Does this character get what he or she deserves?'. From your responses, suggest what kinds of justice you think are at work in the play.

Madness

In Shakespeare's time, attitudes and responses to madness were much harsher and less sympathetic than they are today. Nowadays, doctors rarely use such words as 'mad' or 'lunatic', preferring alternative descriptions; such as 'mentally ill' or 'disturbed'. But Elizabethan and Jacobean audiences had no such modern scruples, and in *King Lear* (and other plays), Shakespeare's language reflects the beliefs of the time. For example, much of Edgar's language, as the madman Poor Tom, is taken from a pamphlet written in 1603 which described how devils were 'cast out of lunatics' (see page 205).

Throughout his career, Shakespeare explored various forms of madness in his plays. He seems to have been particularly interested in madness as an agent of beneficial change. The suffering of mental disturbance could transform characters' views of themselves and others. In the comedies, the 'madness' of love becomes an altered state of consciousness which produces sharper insight. The tragedies offer a more sombre perspective on the effects of madness, but its outcome is also clearer perception. For example, Hamlet (whether his madness be real or feigned) finds calm and understanding after his journey of mental suffering.

Madness in the play is most evident in the portrayal of Lear himself: his mind tormented and unsettled by his experience. But *King Lear* is not simply a psychological depiction of the insanity of an individual. Human madness is reflected in disturbance at two other levels, the natural and the social. The onset of the terrible storm in Act 3 suggests that tempests in nature mirror those in an individual's mind. Lear's abdication of his power and the division of his kingdom would have been seen as acts of political madness by Shakespeare's contemporaries. By tearing up his country, Lear sets off a chain of social frenzy which results in cruelty, blindness, madness and death.

King Lear portrays different types of mental derangement. Lear's madness is that of a selfish, autocratic old man whose will is thwarted. His moral blindness, misjudgements and lack of understanding of himself and others inevitably lead to breakdown: 'O fool, I shall go mad'. As Poor Tom, Edgar puts on the madness of a Bedlam beggar. The Fool's 'madness' is professional, eccentric, witty, exposing weakness and folly: 'May not an ass know when the cart draws the horse?'.

Cornwall and Regan become possessed by the madness of evil in their obsession with Gloucester's punishment and torture: 'Hang him instantly'. Gloucester, near to death, thinks it better to be 'distract' and lose his sorrow in 'wrong imaginations'.

The pattern of Lear's madness

Act 1   Lear's tendency to mental instability is established. He subjects his daughters to a bizarre love trial, banishes his loyal adviser Kent and disowns Cordelia. He reacts with violent curses to Gonerill's challenge to his wilful behaviour.

Act 2   Lear's sanity is undermined by his obsession with 'filial ingratitude', the 'unnatural' behaviour of Gonerill and Regan. Infuriated by Kent's punishment in the stocks, Regan's refusal to speak with him and Gonerill's alliance with her sister, Lear rants impotently of revenge. Fearing the onset of madness, he storms out of Gloucester's castle.

Act 3   Lear rages at the storm, calling for universal destruction. His moods swing violently from raging in the storm to quieter sympathy for those less fortunate than himself: 'Poor naked wretches'. Lear's 'mad' companions, the Fool and Poor Tom, deepen the sense of his decline into insanity. He rips off his clothes ('Off, off you lendings!'), and hallucinates about devilish spirits.

Act 4   A stage direction in Scene 5 indicates *'Enter Lear [mad]'*. Talking with the blinded Gloucester, Lear's language combines sexual loathing with hallucinations about hell and damnation: 'Let copulation thrive … there is the sulphurous pit, burning, scalding, stench, consumption'. Lear's disordered thoughts range over mortality, justice and authority, and erupt in savage emotion: 'And when I have stol'n upon these son-in-laws / Then kill, kill, kill, kill, kill, kill!' At last, reunited with Cordelia, Lear's mental torment ceases.

Act 5   The cruel murder of Cordelia threatens Lear's wits once more: 'Howl, howl, howl, howl!' He dies, his final words suggesting that he is deluding himself with the thought that she lives.

Use the outline above to help you collect quotations from each act to trace the course of Lear's mental state. Choose a style of presentation for your quotations which seems to you powerful and effective, for example an essay, a set of drawings, a short play or set of tableaux.

The politics of *King Lear*

King Lear is firmly rooted in the political and social conditions of Shakespeare's times. The play reflects the political issues which were heatedly debated in Elizabethan and Jacobean England: the divine right of kings, the unity of the kingdom, the changing social order which triggered a growth of conflicting factions and a threatening underclass. From this standpoint, *King Lear* can be seen as a play about the struggle for power, property and inheritance in early seventeenth-century England.

The play opens with Lear portrayed as an absolute monarch who demands unquestioning obedience. In Shakespeare's time, monarchs regarded themselves as ruling on God's behalf. When it attempted to go against her wishes, Queen Elizabeth I reminded Parliament that she was their anointed queen and God's representative on earth. Her successor, King James I, took this belief in the divine right of kings even further. He asserted that it was blasphemous and unlawful to question any action taken by a king. In 1610, he declared to Parliament: 'The state of monarchy is the supremest thing upon the earth; for kings are not only God's lieutenants upon earth, and sit upon God's throne, but even by God himself they are called gods'.

However, such absolute rulers also acknowledged a god-given obligation. It was their sacred duty to keep their kingdom intact. Elizabeth emphasised that she had to answer to God for her government of the realm. She and James shared the conviction that it would be a sin against their divinely given authority to abdicate, or to divide their country. It was an ideology embraced by most of their subjects. So the audience in 1605 probably shared Kent's horror at Lear's decision to throw off the responsibility of kingship and divide his kingdom. They probably also admired Kent's good sense in refusing to share power at the end of the play. To Shakespeare's contemporaries, *King Lear* was a play about how not to rule a country.

The England of Elizabeth and James was a society in transition. The feudal world of medieval times, with its strong allegiances and rigid hierarchy, had virtually collapsed. A newly prosperous gentry and commercial class challenged the power of the king and of an aristocracy divided among itself. Political factions abounded, strongly hinted at in the dangerous rivalry existing between Albany and Cornwall, and gossiped about by Kent and Gloucester as the play opens.

Newly acquired property gave power to a new kind of individual. Powerful men emerged who felt no obligation to the old feudal loyalties. They were men on the make, filled with the spirit of radical individualism, driven by self-interest. Edmond, Gloucester's unscrupulous, illegitimate son, refuses to 'stand in the plague of custom'. In rejecting tradition, he seeks to thrive by his own cunning, mocking the superstitious beliefs of his father, an upholder of the old feudal loyalty to the king. There is no place for an outdated system of chivalry in Edmond's moral scheme. At a different social level, the corrupt Oswald is another example of the 'new man'. His self-serving character is ridiculed by Kent in Act 2 Scene 2 ('such smiling rogues as these …'). Power-seeking, quarrelling aristocrats and the emerging thrusting individualists of Tudor and Jacobean England find their counterparts in Shakespeare's play.

Shakespeare also gives expression to a dispossessed underclass who did not share in the affluence of the times. The enclosure of common fields provoked protest and revolt. What the wealthy classes saw as necessary to more efficient farming, the poor saw as land-grabbing. In the twenty years before the play was written, there were a number of food riots. Shortly after its first performance, serious riots against enclosures took place in the Midlands, including Warwickshire, Shakespeare's home county. Bedlam beggars, the disguise adopted by Edgar, were familiar and deeply worrying figures who roamed: 'from low farms, / Poor pelting villages, sheep-cotes, and mills', pleading for charity.

In *King Lear*, Shakespeare gives expression to crucial political and social issues of his times. Some of these issues remain relevant today. At the end of the twentieth century, the future of the British monarchy and of the union of the countries of the United Kingdom have again become subjects of political debate.

a Talk together about the extent to which the following comment by a government minister is true of the world of the play: 'The relations that hold society together stretch from the top to the bottom. If Crown, Parliament and Church are not respected, neither will be law, judges, policemen nor professors, social workers, nor bosses, managers or foremen. Social disorder follows when respect breaks down.'

b Suggest ways of staging the play to help bring out its relevance to issues in today's society.

The Fool

Fools were popular well before Elizabethan times. In the Middle Ages, jesters were very common as household servants to the rich. They often wore the traditional costume of the coxcomb (jester's cap) with bells, and a motley (multi-coloured) coat. Their role was to entertain with witty words and songs, and to make critical comment on contemporary behaviour. An 'allowed fool', such as Feste in *Twelfth Night*, was able to say what he thought without fear of punishment.

Lear's Fool is 'all-licensed', and so can speak frankly and critically about anything and anyone, especially his master, the king. He acts as a kind of dramatic chorus, an ironic commentator on the action he observes. Although he is threatened with whipping for impertinence, the Fool constantly reminds Lear of his folly. Lear is relentlessly used as the butt of the Fool's barbed comments: 'this fellow has banished two on's daughters and did the third a blessing against his will'; 'thou hast pared thy wit o'both sides and left nothing i'th'middle'; 'I am a fool, thou art nothing'.

The Fool moves easily between different styles of humour: stand-up comedy ('Thou hadst little wit in thy bald crown when thou gav'st thy golden one away'); song ('Fools had ne'er less grace in a year ...'); rhyme or proverb ('Fathers that wear rags / Do make their children blind ...'); and sexual innuendo ('She that's a maid now ...').

The Fool's language seems to be a mixture of sense and nonsense. Attempting to analyse its exact meaning can destroy both its potential humour and its dramatic power. Some of the Fool's words may be puzzling, but all carry significance for Lear's plight. For example, 'So out went the candle, and we were left darkling', spoken as Gonerill begins to undermine Lear's sanity, is eerily prophetic of the blindness and confusion that will follow. The Fool appears in only six scenes. From his very first appearance, his special relationship with Lear is evident. It allows him to escape punishment for his stinging criticisms, and sees him following Lear selflessly into the storm, almost as if he were Lear's *alter ego*, his second, more sane self.

The Fool disappears from the play in Act 3 Scene 6. When Lear says 'And my poor fool is hanged' just before he dies, he may be speaking of the dead Cordelia ('fool' could be a term of endearment). But his sorrowing words create echoes of the Fool (who had 'much pined away' for Cordelia). One production highlighted the relationship between Cordelia and the Fool by beginning with an ominous tableau of them with their necks linked by a hangman's noose.

Every production faces the challenge of how the Fool should be portrayed. In one production he was played as a red-nosed comedian. In another, a woman played the role. How would you portray the Fool if you were directing the play?

Family relationships

At the beginning of the play, Lear and Gloucester both appear to believe that they head successful and happy families. Their illusions do not last long. By the end of the first scene, Lear has torn his family apart. In the opening lines of the second scene, Edmond reveals the plot against his brother which will destroy Gloucester's family.

Shakespeare's sharp dramatic focus is on fathers and their children. Neither family has a mother. The fracturing of bonds between fathers and children is mirrored in the play by the terrible storm in nature, and by the breakdown of society itself. Gloucester, troubled by the discovery of his son Edgar's supposed treachery, expresses that mirror-image: 'Love cools, friendship falls off, brothers divide. In cities, mutinies; in countries, discord; in palaces, treason; and the bond cracked 'twixt son and father'. In *King Lear*, a family problem is a sign of much wider national and cosmic discord.

The family can be viewed as an economic unit which allows one generation to build on the success of the previous one through the inheritance of property and power. In *King Lear*, the riches of a kingdom and an earldom await the heirs of Lear and Gloucester. The issue of inheritance generates great resentment in some children on reaching adulthood. They must await the death of a parent before being able to acquire the family wealth. The letter which Edmond pretends has been written by Edgar makes that resentment clear: 'This policy and reverence of age makes the world bitter to the best of our times, keeps our fortunes from us till our oldness cannot relish them.'

Gonerill and Regan, as well as Edmond, detest such 'aged tyranny', and want to take over the power, wealth and status of their father. Parents sometimes try to control children by manipulating their expectations of inheritance. Lear makes the dangerous mistake of dividing his kingdom between his two ambitious daughters. Gonerill and Regan receive their inheritance and have nothing more to gain by tolerating their father's caprices. Gloucester, however, does not choose to abdicate his role, so his ruthless son Edmond must scheme and plot to replace Edgar as heir, and then seek an opportunity to depose his father.

A family's tragic journey

The royal family, together in the play's opening scene.

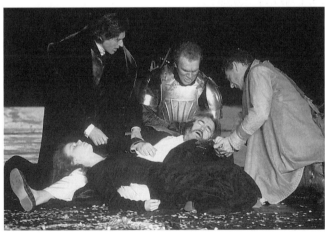

Lear and Cordelia reunited in death at the play's end. The bodies
of Gonerill and Regan lie nearby, but out of sight.

The play begins and ends with the complete royal family on display
before the audience. In contrast to the strong visual image of Lear's
family, established by their appearance together in the opening scene,
the three members of Gloucester's family never appear together on
stage.

The family: a source of love and care

Families satisfy the profound human need for a sense of belonging and for the security of love. Although it may seem obvious that the families of Lear and Gloucester are unsuccessful, they are not totally unloving. Despite the fact that they are both badly treated, Edgar and Cordelia remain selflessly devoted to their fathers.

At the beginning of the play, Lear seems unable to understand and value family love. He demands that his daughters make public statements about how much they love him. His absurd and insensitive command produces glib and over-blown statements from Gonerill and Regan. Lear expects Cordelia to outdo her sisters in flattery, and is angered and humiliated by her refusal to participate. He condemns her for what he believes are harsh words, disregarding all his love for her up to that point. She says that she loves him 'according to my bond', as a daughter ought to love a father. Lear finds this universal statement of family obligation 'untender'. He wants an elaborate and fawning expression of love. Failing to get it, he violently rejects the only one of his children who has real affection for him.

After rejecting Cordelia, Lear announces that he will divide his time between Regan and Gonerill. It does not occur to him that such an action makes him vulnerable. Only respect and love will protect him once he has given up his power. Both Cordelia and Kent suspect the flattery of Gonerill and Regan, and may fear that they do not love or respect Lear enough for him to be safe with them.

A major function of the family is to provide security for its members as they pass through childhood, sickness and old age. Indeed, it is sometimes claimed that one reason why people have children is in order to provide care for themselves in old age. Lear, over eighty years old, certainly expects to be cared for by his daughters after he has given up power. He had hoped to live with Cordelia:

'I loved her most, and thought to set my rest
On her kind nursery.'

Lear later shows a calculating attitude to love when he rates Regan and Gonerill's affection according to the number of his servants they are willing to support. Whoever accepts the larger number must love him the most:

'Thy fifty yet doth double five and twenty,
And thou art twice her love.'

a Talk together about how care of the elderly in modern society can help your understanding of *King Lear*.

b Think about Gonerill and Regan's side of the problem of caring for the aged king. Suggest how they could defend their actions and attitudes.

Lear's descent into madness and his growing awareness of the needs of others helps him to a true understanding of the love which Cordelia has for him. Lear is healed by Cordelia's unconditional love, and finds in it a model for the selfless love of father and daughter. It gives him happiness at the prospect of their imprisonment together, and it cruelly intensifies his agony of grief at her death.

Women in the family

Women often had powerful roles within their families during the sixteenth and seventeenth centuries. However, the power they had outside the family was limited by the rules of inheritance, ingrained traditions, and the prejudiced attitudes of the state, the law and the church. Nonetheless, powerful women were not unknown. King James' mother was Mary Stuart, Queen of Scotland. His immediate predecessor on the English throne was Queen Elizabeth I.

Women in positions of authority caused much consternation in the sixteenth century. In 1558, the year of Elizabeth's accession, John Knox, a Scottish Protestant reformer, issued a pamphlet attacking women rulers. Entitled *First Blast of the Trumpet against the Monstrous Regiment of Women*, it argued that giving women, who are 'weak, frail, impatient, feeble and foolish creatures', any sort of authority was the 'subversion of good order, of all equity and justice'.

By the time *King Lear* was written, attitudes to women in power had been modified by Elizabeth I's success as monarch, but women still had a low status in society. In the play, although Lear's daughters are his heirs, the power and authority of the crown is transferred to their husbands. The daughters are not made queens regnant, monarchs in their own right. Regan and Gonerill are strong and influential figures, but have to wield that influence through their husbands. Consequently, Gonerill has to goad Albany into action when he has doubts about how to react to the political crisis. She knows it would be difficult, if not impossible, for her to act alone.

Gonerill and Regan both want Edmond, not just as a lover, but as a consort. Their reasons may be entirely personal, or may be connected with their appraisal of his skills as a commander and ruler. Although all three princesses play authoritative roles in the preparations for battle, it is Albany and Edmond who lead the British army. Cordelia acts as commander-in-chief of the invading French army, but has been invested with that authority by her husband (Act 4 Scene 3, lines 25–6).

Lear's wife, the mother of his daughters and the Queen of Britain, is dead before the play begins. In the Gloucester family, too, both the mothers are absent from the play. Edmond's mother is only mentioned when he or his father refer lewdly to his conception. There are no references to Edgar's mother.

Cordelia, Gonerill and Regan. What family likenesses and differences can you see in this portrayal of the three sisters? Think about how far the picture matches your own image of the sisters, and suggest how you would like to see them portrayed on stage (actors, costumes, movements, style of speech, and so on).

Sons and brothers

The sub-plot of Gloucester and his two sons very obviously increases the dramatic effect of the main plot of Lear and his daughters. The good and evil qualities of the king's daughters are reflected in Edgar's struggles to protect his father, and Edmond's schemes to harm him. The play's exploration of family life offers every new production a challenge in how to portray the brothers.

Brothers can be remarkably similar or very different in appearance and character. There are obvious and stark contrasts between the two Gloucester half-brothers. For example, Edgar plays a number of roles: a gullible dupe who believes his brother's false story; a madman, as Poor Tom; a choric commentator on suffering ('ripeness is all'); a defender of right as he slays both Edmond and Oswald. In contrast, Edmond seems to be unremittingly devious, seeking whatever will serve his own interests. Only in the closing minutes of the play, near to death, is he prompted to do good, and unsuccessfully tries to prevent the deaths of Lear and Cordelia.

'My name is Edgar, and thy father's son.' Edgar reveals his identity to his dying brother. The wheel has come full circle, and Edmond pays the price for his wrongdoing.

The language of *King Lear*

1 Lear's changing language

Lear's first words in the play are an abrupt order to Gloucester, 'Attend the lords of France and Burgundy'. Throughout the opening scene, his language bristles with the commands and imperious statements and questions of a king confident of his unshakeable authority. Even in his madness Lear strives to dictate to the elements, instructing the storm, 'Blow, winds, and crack your cheeks!'. At the end of the play he is still giving orders, but his tone has radically changed into a polite request, 'Pray you, undo this button. Thank you, sir'. His final words, 'Look there, look there', are an impassioned plea for confirmation that Cordelia still lives.

Although Lear speaks the language of power, there is great variation in his speech. For example, his dialogues with the Fool are quite different from those with Gonerill and Regan. As the play progresses, he learns through his suffering that a king's role is not simply to command. When he is reunited with Cordelia, his language has changed completely.

Either: Working in pairs, take parts and speak the following aloud:

- the dialogue between Lear and Cordelia in Act 1 Scene 1, lines 77–114
- the dialogue between Lear and Cordelia in Act 5 Scene 3, lines 3–26
- all that Lear says in Act 5 Scene 3, lines 231–85

When you have spoken the lines, talk together about how you think Lear's language changes in these three scenes.

Or: Choose two or three major characters and trace the way in which Lear speaks to them throughout the play, noting any changes in his manner of addressing them.

2 Sight and blindness

Lear banishes Kent with 'Out of my sight!'. Kent's reply, 'See better, Lear ...', identifies Lear's moral blindness, his lack of self-knowledge and understanding. There is a terrible literalness in Gonerill's 'Pluck out his eyes', and in Cornwall's brutal execution of that order, 'Upon these eyes of thine I'll set my foot'. The many images of sight and blindness which pervade the play sharply underscore and emphasise the dramatic effect of that horrifying statement.

Gloucester talks ironically of not needing 'spectacles' to read Edgar's traitorous letter. The villainous Edmond can clearly 'see the business'. Lear speaks of 'Old fond eyes' which threaten to shed tears, and the physical pain and suffering experienced by Gloucester as a result of his blinding bring him insight into his past errors, 'I stumbled when I saw'. His new-found compassionate awareness of the nature of the world is vividly expressed, 'I see it feelingly'.

Collect four or five references to sight, eyes or blindness from each act. Work out a powerful way of presenting your collection to illustrate the importance of sight and blindness in *King Lear*. For example, you could write an essay, make a large diagram or wall display, or rehearse and present a short play.

3 Animal imagery

King Lear resonates with the imagery of animals. Lear likens his daughters' cruelty to that of predatory birds and beasts. He calls Gonerill a 'Detested kite' whose ingratitude is 'sharper than a serpent's tooth'. Her face is 'wolvish', her tongue 'serpent-like'. In his madness he sees Gonerill and Regan as 'pelican daughters', cruelly feeding on his flesh and blood. Losing his temper, Lear calls Oswald a 'whoreson dog' and a 'cur'. As Poor Tom, Edgar 'eats the swimming frog, the toad, the tadpole, the wall-newt … swallows the old rat and the ditch dog'. He describes himself as 'hog in sloth, fox in stealth, wolf in greediness, dog in madness, lion in prey'.

Set against the long catalogue of the natural world (dragon, worm, beetles, mouse, sea-monster, snail, rats, vermin, bears, monkey, swine, adder), human behaviour in the play sinks to the level of the 'poor, bare, forked animal'. Gloucester's vivid image reduces humans to insignificant insects, 'As flies to wanton boys are we to the gods / They kill us for their sport.'

Collect as many animal references as you can. Work out a way of presenting your collection that you find satisfying.

4 Disease and pain

The political and moral disruptions which result from Lear's division of his kingdom are echoed in recurring images of pain and disease, of bodies racked and tortured. Most obviously, Lear's madness and Gloucester's blinding illustrate the theme of mental and physical suffering.

The language of the play is studded with references to sickness and ailments. Kent identifies Lear's banishing of Cordelia as a 'foul disease'.

Lear views the Fool's criticisms as a 'pestilent gall' (an infected irritant). He curses Gonerill with unhealthy vapours ('fen-sucked fogs'), hoping that they blister her. On both ungrateful daughters he wishes 'all the plagues that in the pendulous air hang'. To Lear, Gonerill is 'a disease that's in my flesh', 'a boil / A plague-sore, or embossèd carbuncle'. In his madness, Lear's ravings trigger his disgust at the thought of sexually transmitted diseases, 'There's hell, there's darkness, there is the sulphurous pit, burning, scalding, stench, consumption'.

Although disease imagery runs through the play, it is partly counterbalanced by the language of healing. Reunited with Lear in Act 4, Cordelia seeks to return him to health, 'restoration hang / Thy medicine on my lips'.

Identify six to eight examples of images of disease and pain. Consider each example in turn, and suggest how far you think it could apply to:

- the state of Lear's England
- Lear's mental state
- his moral state
- his physical state.

5 Christian or pre-Christian?

There is much argument about whether *King Lear* is a Christian play. Those who see it as Christian see Lear redeemed by the 'crucifixion' of his suffering. They identify Cordelia as a symbol of Christian redemption, almost Christ-like. She is a healer of suffering, a purger of ills and sins. Her reconciliation with her father helps to restore his wits. Her language continually affirms such Christian qualities as tolerance and understanding: 'blest', 'virtues', 'aidant', 'remediate', 'love', 'goodness', 'cure', 'restoration', 'repair', 'pity', 'benediction'. When she returns at the head of an army to aid Lear, her words echo those of Jesus, 'O dear father / It is thy business that I go about' (Act 4 Scene 3).

However, there is much evidence in *King Lear* of a pre-Christian world. Characters do not appeal to a Christian god, but to the sun, Hecate, Apollo and Jupiter. Lear proclaims his faith in 'high-judging Jove'. Gloucester's world is beset by superstitious beliefs in the 'late eclipses in the sun and moon'. Edmond puts his faith in Nature as his goddess. Gloucester, Albany, Cordelia and Kent constantly appeal to the gods as they try to make sense of the apparently arbitrary nature of fortune and justice which they dispense, 'That shows you are above / You justicers'.

Work in two groups. One group collects non-Christian references in the play. The other group identifies possible allusions to a Christian world. Organise a discussion on what a production of *King Lear* gains and loses from being set in a pre-Christian environment.

6 Nothing

The word 'nothing' resounds throughout the play. Cordelia uses it first, saying 'Nothing, my lord' in answer to Lear's love test. She has nothing to say, no flattering words to embellish the dutiful love she feels for her father. Lear's response adds a new meaning, 'Nothing will come of nothing'. If she does not declare her love, she will inherit nothing. The word will shift its meaning constantly in the mouth of each character: no words, no wealth, no meaning, no brains, no identity.

Gloucester will reward Edmond ('It shall lose thee nothing') for his false loyalty. Lear criticises the Fool's joking advice, 'This is nothing, fool'. His criticism is returned with a sharp twist of meaning, 'thou hast pared thy wit o'both sides and left nothing i'th'middle'. The Fool gives the word yet another interpretation, loss of identity: 'I am a fool, thou art nothing'. It is a meaning which is echoed as Edgar discards his true personality, 'Edgar I nothing am'.

Gonerill and Regan chillingly remind Lear that his former power will be reduced to nothing, 'What need you five and twenty? ten? or five? ... What need one?'. The consequences of Lear's rash act are devastatingly brought home to him, although 'nothing' remains unspoken. Many of the characters will be left with nothing at the play's end. In the most literal sense, they will be brought to nothing, losing life itself.

Write a paragraph giving your response to the claim that: 'The essence of the play can be summarised in Lear's five words, "Nothing will come of nothing".

7 Plain speaking

King Lear strikingly explores the differences between speaking sincerely and insincerely. Some characters' private thoughts quite clearly do not match their public voices. Cordelia recognises that her sisters speak untruthfully in Lear's 'love test', but she refuses to speak dishonestly, 'I want that glib and oily art / To speak and purpose not'. Yet elsewhere, Gonerill and Regan's language is plain and direct, even though the duplicitous nature of their scheming pervades the play.

Kent is banished for his plain speaking, 'his offence, honesty'. He returns as a character still committed to speaking candidly and bluntly. Criticised by Cornwall for 'bluntness' and a 'saucy roughness', Kent draws attention to the contrast between speaking falsely and speaking honestly as he puts on an elaborately affected style of speech (Act 2, Scene 2, line 95).

Edmond uses lies to prey on a 'credulous father' and his 'foolish honesty'. Later, Edmond uses his cunning to 'stuff his [Cornwall's] suspicions more fully'. Even the virtuous Edgar, disguised as Poor Tom, lies to his blinded father. But his motivation is benign, 'Why I do trifle thus with his despair / Is done to cure it'.

At the end of *King Lear*, Edgar urges plain speaking, 'Speak what we feel, not what we ought to say'. Consider each character in turn, and assess to what extent they have spoken honestly throughout the play. Suggest reasons why the characters choose to hide their true thoughts.

8 Verse or prose?

How did Shakespeare decide whether his characters should speak in verse or prose? A rough answer is that he followed the stage conventions of his time. His theatre audiences generally expected to hear plays in verse. However, it was conventional for prose to be used by low status characters, for comedy, to express madness, and in letters.

So today, a popular belief about Shakespeare's language is that his high-status characters speak verse and his lower-status characters use prose. Those who hold this belief sometimes argue that verse is particularly appropriate to the noble, 'serious' thoughts of aristocrats, and to heightened and passionate feelings, in contrast to the everyday or comic thoughts of 'ordinary' people. But is this belief true of *King Lear*?

Shakespeare never followed any convention slavishly, and there are plenty of exceptions to the verse/prose conventions. For example, Gloucester and Edmond's conversation in Act 1 Scene 2, Lear's dialogues with the Fool, and his conversations with Poor Tom and the blinded Gloucester. In his madness, Lear uses both prose and verse.

Turn at random to three or four pages in the play and suggest why prose may be appropriate at such moments.

Staging the play

King Lear was probably performed many times during Shakespeare's lifetime. The first record of a performance is 'before the King's majesty at Whitehall' on the 26 December 1606. What would King James have made of a Christmas entertainment showing the spectacle of a mad king who divided and gave away his kingdom? He probably enjoyed it, partly because it confirmed his view that a divided kingdom was the utmost political folly, and partly because 26 December was traditionally a day on which human foolishness and the virtue of enduring hardship with patience were celebrated.

How King James 'watched' *King Lear* would have been greatly affected by the same factors which influenced Shakespeare as he wrote it (see pages 202–05), namely the prevailing political and cultural assumptions of the times. Since those first performances, all subsequent productions have mirrored in some way the interests and anxieties, pre-occupations, beliefs and values of their times. There is no one 'right way' to perform or interpret *King Lear*. Each performance reflects the political, religious, literary or aesthetic ideologies of the times.

After the English Civil War and the execution of King Charles I, audiences had little stomach for the harshness of Shakespeare's play. In 1681, the dramatist Nahum Tate rewrote it with a happy ending, and produced a version which lasted on stage for over one hundred and fifty years. Tate cut the Fool, invented a trusted woman friend for Cordelia (whom he married off to Edgar), and ensured that Lear, Kent and Gloucester survived into the happy retirement of old age, leaving Cordelia and Edgar to rule the kingdom.

Not until the nineteenth century did Shakespeare's intended version of the play enjoy real stage success over Tate's happy ending version. But, even then, the influence of political considerations on drama and theatre can be clearly seen. During the mental derangement of King George III, performances of *King Lear* were suspended because the play came too close to reality for comfort.

Nineteenth-century productions were increasingly concerned with spectacle. Large casts, lavish costumes and monumental sets were used in an attempt to give historical accuracy to the play. The problem was that 'historical accuracy' is not a concept which lends itself happily to *King Lear*. Quite simply, no one knows where or when Shakespeare intended it to be set (and it is possible that he had no specific time or place in mind except 'long-ago England'). Famous productions set the play in Saxon times or among the ancient Druids or at Stonehenge.

The twentieth century has seen attempts to return to what Shakespeare originally wrote (given the problem of quarto/Folio versions, see page 232), and to face squarely the bleakness and horror of Shakespeare's vision. In a century which has given full expression to the terrors of mechanised warfare and human cruelty, *King Lear* has become one of the most frequently performed of all Shakespeare's plays, and many people argue that it is Shakespeare's greatest play. Virtually all modern productions attempt to bring out the play's contemporary significance and relevance.

One of the most celebrated versions was Peter Brook's at Stratford in 1962, which emphasised the bleakness of existence and its pain and suffering. For example, there was no help from servants for Gloucester after his blinding (see page 132, Activity 2), and Edmond's line 'Some good I mean to do' was cut (Act 5, Scene 3, line 217).

Use the illustrations throughout this edition to help you work out how you would stage *King Lear*. Consider costumes, historical period, set, and so on.

As this painting of an eighteenth-century production shows, the play was performed in 'modern' dress. Lear is wearing contemporary court dress.

This 1936 production opened with great ceremony to the blast of trumpets.
It began at line 29 of Scene 1.

This 1981 Hungarian production set the play on the site of an abandoned
factory and railway. The loudspeakers and the stark set emphasise the director's
intention to present the play as a political parable about authority in
Eastern Europe in the 1980s.

A still from the 1962 film directed by Peter Brook. Filming Shakespeare gives a director opportunities which are not available in stage productions.

Shakespeare's plays are popular with audiences he could never have imagined. This photograph is a still from the Japanese film *Ran*, which sets *King Lear* in the traditional culture of Japan.

Quarto and Folio editions

Two different versions of the *King Lear* script exist. A quarto version was printed in 1608. The Folio version was published in 1623, when all Shakespeare's plays were gathered together in one large volume, the First Folio. The words 'quarto' and 'Folio' refer to the size of the pages in the two editions.

The quarto may be an illegal publication based on a stolen copy of Shakespeare's working script. Another suggestion is that the boy actors playing Gonerill and Regan pieced together a version from memory. The quarto contains hundreds of printing errors, but the Folio version is well printed, containing few obvious mistakes. The Folio seems to have been based on a copy of the play carefully prepared for publication or performance.

The Folio cuts out three hundred lines included in the quarto, but adds one hundred new lines, altering the way in which characters are shown, the overall structure of the play, and the emotional force of certain scenes. The Folio presents a more sombre and bleak version of the play. An entire scene disappears. The French invasion is played down.

No one can be certain why Shakespeare altered his play so much. Perhaps he was anxious not to offend the authorities in case they decided to impose censorship, and so cut the lines calling the king a fool. He may have felt that he could intensify dramatic effect by making the play more harsh. Perhaps he shortened the play in order to prepare a touring version. But no one knows whether the Folio version was Shakespeare's final word on *King Lear*. Maybe he intended to reinstate the lines which he had cut earlier, but died before he could do so. It is quite possible that the Folio version was prepared for publication by someone else, not by Shakespeare himself.

Stage productions usually combine elements from both versions of the play. This edition uses the Folio version, because it may be Shakespeare's final thoughts on the play. On the following three pages and throughout this edition you will find lines from the quarto version which do not appear in the Folio. In each case, they are an invitation to you to decide for yourself whether you would include them in your own production of the play. As you make your decisions, bear in mind the effect they will have on characterisation, dramatic effect and mood.

The mock trial of Gonerill (following line 14 in Act 3 Scene 6)

Lear conducts a trial to 'arraign' (bring before a court) Gonerill and Regan. He instructs Edgar to take the part of a judge in robes, the Fool to be his partner ('yoke-fellow'), and Kent to join them as a member of the 'commission' (panel of judges). A 'joint-stool', a low stool made by a carpenter, stands in for Gonerill.

EDGAR The foul fiend bites my back.

FOOL. He's mad that trusts in the tameness of a wolf, a horse's health, a boy's love, or a whore's oath.

LEAR It shall be done; I will arraign them straight.
    [*To Edgar*] Come, sit thou here, most learnèd justicer.
    [*To the Fool*] Thou, sapient sir, sit here. – No, you she-foxes –

EDGAR Look where he stands and glares! Want'st thou eyes at trial, madam?
    [*Sings*] Come o'er the bourn, Bessy, to me.

FOOL [*Sings*]   Her boat hath a leak
        And she must not speak
        Why she dares not come over to thee.

EDGAR The foul fiend haunts poor Tom in the voice of a nightingale. Hoppe-dance cries in Tom's belly for two white herring. Croak not, black angel! I have no food for thee.

KENT How do you, Sir? Stand you not so amazed.
    Will you lie down and rest upon the cushions?

LEAR I'll see their trial first. – Bring in their evidence.
    [*To Edgar*] Thou robèd man of justice, take thy place.
    [*To the Fool*] And thou, his yoke-fellow of equity,
    Bench by his side. [To Kent] You are o'th'commission;
    Sit you too.

EDGAR Let us deal justly.
    Sleepest or wakest thou, jolly shepherd?
        Thy sheep be in the corn;
    And for one blast of thy minikin mouth
        Thy sheep shall take no harm.
    Purr, the cat, is grey.

LEAR Arraign her first; 'tis Gonerill. I here take my oath before this honourable assembly, she kicked the poor king her father.

FOOL Come hither, mistress. Is your name Gonerill?

LEAR She cannot deny it.

FOOL Cry you mercy, I took you for a joint-stool.

LEAR And here's another whose warped looks proclaim
    What store her heart is made on. – Stop her there!
    Arms, arms, sword, fire! Corruption in the place!
    False justicer, why hast thou let her 'scape?

The lessons of suffering (following the last line in Act 3 Scene 6)

The quarto includes a soliloquy for Edgar after Lear has been carried off to Dover. Edgar acknowledges that the king's suffering is far greater than his own. He plans to watch events and to reveal ('bewray') his true identity when the charges against him have been disproved.

EDGAR   When we our betters see bearing our woes,
   We scarcely think our miseries our foes.
   Who alone suffers, suffers most i'th'mind,
   Leaving free things and happy shows behind.
   But then the mind much sufferance doth o'erskip,
   When grief hath mates, and bearing, fellowship.
   How light and portable my pain seems now,
   When that which makes me bend makes the king bow.
   He childed as I fathered. Tom, away!
   Mark the high noises, and thyself bewray
   When false opinion, whose wrong thoughts defile thee,
   In thy just reproof repeals and reconciles thee.
   What will hap more tonight, safe 'scape the king!
   Lurk, lurk!

An omitted scene (after Act 4 Scene 2)

The quarto includes a complete scene in which Kent and a Gentleman discuss the French invasion of Britain. The Gentleman describes Cordelia's compassionate reaction to news of her father's plight, and how Lear's sense of shame makes him unwilling to see her.

KENT Why the King of France is so suddenly gone back, know you no
   reason?
GENTLEMAN Something he left imperfect in the state which since his
   coming forth is thought of, which imports to the kingdom so much
   fear and danger that his personal return was most required and
   necessary.
KENT Who hath he left behind him general?
GENTLEMAN The Marshal of France, Monsieur La Far.
KENT Did your letters pierce the queen to any demonstration of grief?
GENTLEMAN Ay, sir. She took them, read them in my presence,
   And now and then an ample tear trilled down
   Her delicate cheek. It seemed she was a queen
   Over her passion, who most rebel-like
   Sought to be king o'er her.
KENT   O, then it moved her?

GENTLEMAN Not to a rage. Patience and sorrow strove
        Who should express her goodliest. You have seen
        Sunshine and rain at once; her smiles and tears
        Were like a better way; those happy smilets
        That played on her ripe lip seemed not to know
        What guests were in her eyes; which parted thence
        As pearls from diamonds dropped. In brief.
        Sorrow would be a rarity most beloved
        If all could so become it.

KENT Made she no verbal question?

GENTLEMAN Faith, once or twice she heaved the name of father
        Pantingly forth, as if it pressed her heart;
        Cried 'Sisters, sisters! Shame of ladies! Sisters!
        Kent! Father! Sisters! What, i'th'storm? i'th'night?
        Let pity not be believed!' There she shook
        The holy water from her heavenly eyes,
        And clamour moistened. Then away she started
        To deal with grief alone.

KENT   It is the stars,
        The stars above us, govern our conditions,
        Else one self mate and make could not beget
        Such different issues. You spoke not with her since?

GENTLEMAN No.

KENT Was this before the king returned?

GENTLEMAN   No, since.

KENT Well, sir, the poor distressèd Lear's i'th'town,
        Who sometime in his better tune remembers
        What we are come about and by no means
        Will yield to see his daughter.

GENTLEMAN   Why, good sir?

KENT A sovereign shame so elbows him: his own unkindness
        That stripped her from his benediction, turned her
        To foreign casualties, gave her dear rights
        To his dog-hearted daughters – these things sting
        His mind so venomously that burning shame
        Detains him from Cordelia.

GENTLEMAN Alack, poor gentleman!

KENT Of Albany's and Cornwall's powers you heard not?

GENTLEMAN 'Tis so. They are afoot.

KENT Well, sir, I'll bring you to our master, Lear,
        And leave you to attend him. Some dear cause
        Will in concealment wrap me up awhile.
        When I am known aright, you shall not grieve
        Lending me this acquaintance. I pray you, go
        Along with me.

William Shakespeare 1564–1616

1564 Born Stratford-upon-Avon, eldest son of John and Mary Shakespeare.
1582 Marries Anne Hathaway of Shottery, near Stratford.
1583 Daughter, Susanna, born.
1585 Twins, son and daughter, Hamnet and Judith, born.
1592 First mention of Shakespeare in London. Robert Greene, another playwright, described Shakespeare as 'an upstart crow beautified with our feathers…'. Greene seems to have been jealous of Shakespeare. He mocked Shakespeare's name, calling him 'the only Shake-scene in the country' (presumably because Shakespeare was writing successful plays).
1595 A shareholder in 'The Lord Chamberlain's Men', an acting company that became extremely popular.
1596 Son Hamnet dies, aged eleven.
       Father, John, granted arms (acknowledged as a gentleman).
1597 Bought New Place, the grandest house in Stratford.
1598 Acted in Ben Jonson's *Every Man in His Humour*.
1599 Globe Theatre opens on Bankside. Performances in the open air.
1601 Father, John, dies.
1603 James I grants Shakespeare's company a royal patent: 'The Lord Chamberlain's Men' became 'The King's Men' and played about twelve performances each year at court.
1607 Daughter, Susanna, marries Dr John Hall.
1608 Mother, Mary, dies.
1609 'The King's Men' begin performing indoors at Blackfriars Theatre.
1610 Probably returned from London to live in Stratford.
1616 Daughter, Judith, marries Thomas Quiney.
       Dies. Buried in Holy Trinity Church, Stratford-upon-Avon.

The plays and poems
(no one knows exactly when he wrote each play)

1589–1595 *The Two Gentlemen of Verona, The Taming of the Shrew, First, Second and Third Parts of King Henry VI, Titus Andronicus, King Richard III, The Comedy of Errors, Love's Labour's Lost, A Midsummer Night's Dream, Romeo and Juliet, King Richard II* (and the long poems *Venus and Adonis* and *The Rape of Lucrece*).

1596–1599 *King John, The Merchant of Venice, First and Second Parts of King Henry IV, The Merry Wives of Windsor, Much Ado About Nothing, King Henry V, Julius Caesar* (and probably the *Sonnets*).

1600–1605 *As You Like It, Hamlet, Twelfth Night, Troilus and Cressida, Measure for Measure, Othello, All's Well That Ends Well, Timon of Athens, King Lear.*

1606–1611 *Macbeth, Antony and Cleopatra, Pericles, Coriolanus, The Winter's Tale, Cymbeline, The Tempest.*

1613 *King Henry VIII, The Two Noble Kinsmen* (both probably with John Fletcher).

1623 Shakespeare's plays published as a collection (now called the First Folio).